1•2•3 Shapes

Learning Shape Activities for Young Children

Edited By Gayle Bittinger
Illustrated By Susan Dahlman
Cover Illustration By Marion Hopping Ekberg

Totline® Publications
A Division of Frank Schaffer Publications, Inc.
Torrance, California

Totline Publications would like to thank the following people for their contributions to this book: *Gillian Adams, Newark, NJ; Janice Bodenstedt, Jackson, MI; Rita Choiniere, East Providence, RI; Vicki Claybrook, Kennewick, WA; Barbara Conahan, Hazleton, PA; Marjorie Debowy, Stony Brook, NY; Barbara Dunn, Hollidaysburg, PA; Rita Galloway, Harlingen, TX; Lanette Gutierrez, Olympia, WA; Judy Hall, Wytheville, VA; Lindsay Hall, Wytheville, VA; Shelley Hansen, Wichita, KS; Judith Hanson, Newton Falls, OH; Barbara H. Jackson, Denton, TX; Ellen Javernick, Loveland, CO; Karen Kilimnik, Philadelphia, PA; Neoma Kreuter, El Dorado Springs, MO; Brenda MacQuillian, Crownsville, MD; Barb Mazzochi, Villa Park, IL; Kathy McCullough, Everett, WA; Joleen Meier, Marietta, GA; Susan A. Miller, Kutztown, PA; Laura H. Nass, Twin Falls, ID; Susan M. Paprocki, Northbrook, IL; Jeanne Petty, Camden, DE; Lois E. Putnam, Pilot Mountain, NC; Beverly Qualheim, Marquette, MI; Deborah A. Roessel, Flemington, NJ; Michelle Sears, Glen Falls, NY; Vicki Shannon, Napton, MO; Betty Silkunas, Lansdale, PA; Janet Sloey, Manchester, MO; Evelyn Smith, Columbus, OH; Priscilla M. Starrett, Warren, PA; Diane Thom, Maple Valley, WA; Cathi Ulbright, Wooster, OH; Nancy C. Windes, Denver, CO; Jodi Winston, Everett, WA; Jean Woods, Tulsa, OK.*

Editorial Staff:
   Managing Editor: Kathleen Cubley
   Contributing Editors: Susan Hodges, Elizabeth McKinnon,
      Jean Warren
   Copy Editor: Kris Fulsaas
   Proofreader: Mae Rhodes
   Editorial Assistants: Kate Ffolliott, Erica West

Design and Production Staff:
   Art Managers: Uma Kukathas, Jill Lustig
   Book Design/Layout: Sarah Ness
   Cover Design/Layout: Brenda Mann Harrison
   Cover Illustration: Marion Hopping Ekberg
   Production Manager: JoAnna Haffner

ISBN 1-57029-006-7

Library of Congress Catalog Number 94-060690

Printed in the United States of America
Published by: Totline® Publications

Business Office: 23740 Hawthorne Blvd.
   Torrance, CA 90505

Introduction

Every day is Shape Day for young children. Shapes are everywhere, making them the perfect beginning teaching tool. There are shapes to identify, shapes to count, shapes to match, and shapes to sort. In every area of learning, shapes can be used easily and effectively to teach basic skills.

1•2•3 Shapes contains activities for learning about shapes and using shapes to teach beginning concepts. The activities in the first eight chapters are grouped by individual shapes and include suggestions for art, learning games, language, science, movement, music, and snacks. The final chapter contains activities that can be used for all shapes as well as activities that are designed for working with more than one shape.

We invite you to look through this exciting collection of shape ideas. Then help your children use shapes as a bridge to fun and learning.

Contents

Fun With Circles 7

Fun With Squares 27

Fun With Triangles.....................47

Fun With Rectangles 67

Fun With Ovals..........................87

Fun With Diamonds 99

Fun With Hearts 111

Fun With Stars 123

Fun With Many Shapes.............135

Fun With Circles

Caterpillar Mural

Pour small amounts of tempera paint into shallow containers. Cut sponges into circles. Hang a long piece of butcher paper on a wall at your children's eye level. Give each child a paper plate and a sponge circle. Let the children dip their sponges into the paint, then press them all over their plates. Allow the paint to dry. To make a mural, hook the plates together in a row with brass paper fasteners. (See illustration.) Add a plate with a caterpillar face drawn on it and two pipe cleaner antennae. Attach the paper-plate caterpillar to the butcher paper, arranging the plates so that the caterpillar appears to be moving.

Spinning Circle Art

Cut various sizes of circles out of colorful paper. Make a hole slightly off center in each one. Let the children each select several of the circles and arrange them one on top of the other from largest to smallest. Fasten each child's circles together by lining up the holes and inserting a brass paper fastener. Then let the children turn their circles around the fasteners to create spinning art.

Painted Circles

Collect some plastic bubble wrap. (Plastic bubble wrap is available where packaging materials are sold.) Cut 8-inch circles out of the wrap. Tape the circles to a table. Let your children paint on the bubble wrap. As each child finishes, press a sheet of paper over his or her design to reveal lots of little circles. Rinse off the bubble-wrap circles and let your children paint them again.

Circle Cookies

Give your children large cookie shapes cut from light-brown construction paper. Let them make "cookie sprinkles" by using a hole punch to punch small circles out of other colors of paper. Have the children brush glue all over their cookie shapes and then add the colorful circle sprinkles.

Circle Prints

Set out several different kinds of small balls such as foam balls, tennis balls, and rubber balls. Have your children dip the balls into tempera paint and then press them onto pieces of construction paper. Ask them to name the shapes of the prints on their papers. Let them try making prints with each type of ball.

Variation: Instead of using balls, let your children make prints with partially blown-up balloons.

Colorful Crayon Circles

Chop a variety of colors of old peeled crayons into ¼-inch pieces and place them in the baking cups of an old muffin tin. Heat the crayons at 250 degrees for 5 minutes or until the crayon pieces just begin to melt together. Turn off the oven and leave the muffin tin in it. Allow the crayons to cool in the oven before removing them from the muffin tin. Let your children draw pictures with the Colorful Crayon Circles.

Wheel Art

Cut car and truck shapes (minus the wheels) out of various colors of construction paper. On large sheets of construction paper, draw simple roads. Give each of your children several of the car and truck shapes and one of the large sheets of construction paper. Let the children glue their shapes onto the roads on their papers. Then have them glue on round button "wheels" to complete their pictures.

Variation: Instead of using buttons for wheels, let your children attach self-stick circles or construction-paper circles.

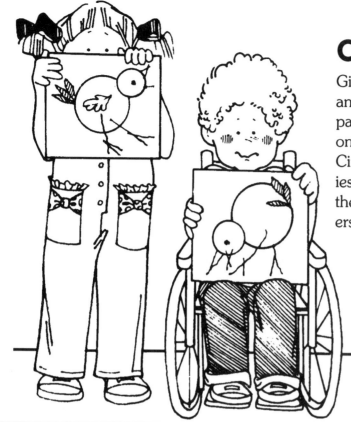

Circle Birds

Give each of your children a large circle and a small circle cut out of construction paper. Have the children glue their circles on sheets of construction paper to create Circle Birds, using the large circles for bodies and the small circles for heads. Then let them decorate their birds with felt-tip markers and glued-on feathers.

Circle Snowpals

Make a snowpal for each of your children by stapling a small paper plate to the top of a large paper plate. Cut small circles out of black construction paper. Let the children decorate their snowpals by gluing the circles onto the paper plates.

Variation: Have your children glue on buttons instead of paper circles.

Poker Chip Patterns

Set out two piles of different-colored poker chips such as red and white. Place some of the poker chips in a row in a simple pattern. For example: red-white, red-white. Have one of your children use more poker chips to repeat the pattern under your row. As the child's skill in duplicating simple patterns increases, make the pattern more difficult or add another color. For example: red-red-white, red-red-white or red-blue-white, red-blue-white.

Lid Puzzle

Collect several round metal lids of various sizes. Using a hammer and a nail, pound two holes, about 1 inch apart, in the middle of each lid and attach a pipe-cleaner handle. Place the lids on top of a round piece of cardboard or plastic foam. Draw around each lid, then cut out and discard the circle shapes. Give a child the piece of cardboard with the holes in it and the lids. Have the child put each lid into the appropriate hole.

Button Sorting

Collect a variety of buttons, including buttons that are not round. Place the buttons on a tray. Set out the tray, a bowl, and a box. Have your children sort through the buttons and place the round buttons in the bowl and the buttons that are not round in the box.

Coin Sorting

Place several pennies, nickels, dimes, and quarters into a coin purse. Sit with one of your children and give him or her the purse. Let the child remove the coins one at a time, name them, and place them in four separate piles.

Variation: Cut slits in the lids of four small boxes to make "banks." Label the banks by taping on a penny, a nickel, a dime, and a quarter. Let the child put matching coins into each bank.

Lacing Plates

For each of your children, punch holes 1 to 2 inches apart around the rim of a paper plate. Tie a long piece of yarn to one of the holes. Tape the other end of the yarn to make a "needle." Give the children the plates and show them how to lace the yarn in and out of the holes.

Puzzle Plates

Give each of your children a paper plate with a solid color painted around the rim. Let the children use felt-tip markers to draw pictures on their plates. Then cut each plate into three to six puzzle pieces (depending on the age of the child). Give the children their puzzle pieces and plain paper plates to use as puzzle holders. Let the children put their own puzzles together. Then have them exchange puzzles with friends.

Making Snowpals

From white felt, cut three large circles, three medium-sized circles, and three small circles. Then cut three top-hat shapes out of black felt. Have the children place the large circles in a row on a flannelboard. Let them place the medium-sized circles on top of the large circles. Then have them place the small circles above the medium-sized circles. Let the children add the top hats to make snowpals. Then mix up all the circles and hats and let the children make the snowpals all over again.

Pie Puzzles

Cut three identical 9-inch circles out of heavy paper. Decorate each circle with a different color to make three different kinds of "pie." Then cut one pie in half, one in fourths and one in eighths. Mix up the pieces and let the children put them together in various ways to make three whole pies.

Variation: For younger children, set out the pieces for one pie at a time.

Circle-Kid Finger Puppets

Cut 5-inch circles out of large white index cards and make two finger holes near the bottom of each circle. Give one to each of your children. Let the children glue on precut construction-paper eye and mouth shapes. Then show them how to stick two of their fingers through the holes in their puppets to make legs.

Circle Puppets

For each of your children, cut two 4-inch circles out of self-stick paper. Cut yarn into short pieces. Remove the backings from the self-stick circles. Give each child one of the circles and some yarn pieces. Have the children place the yarn pieces around the top halves of the sticky sides of their circles to make hair. Place a second circle on top of each child's first circle, sticky sides together, with a craft stick in between for a handle. Have the children use permanent felt-tip markers to add facial features to their Circle Puppets. Let the children use their puppets to talk with one another.

What Is a Circle?

Read the following rhyme to your children. You may wish to have pictures of the items mentioned in the rhyme to show your children as they are named.

Now what is a circle?
Where can it be found?
I know what it looks like,
It goes round and round.

It could be a flying disk
Or the top of a cake,
It could be a pizza
Or a cookie we baked.

It could be the tire
On a brand-new car,
It could be a button
Or the lid of a jar.

Now what is a circle?
Well, you'll just have to guess.
A circle is something
A little like this.

(Form circle with thumb and forefinger.)

Vicki Claybrook

Circle Families

Give each of your children a large sheet of construction paper. Set out construction-paper circles of varying sizes and colors. Ask each child in turn to name the members of his or her family and let him or her select an appropriately sized circle to represent each member. Have the children glue their circles on their papers. Let them use crayons or felt-tip markers to add arms, legs, facial features, and other details. Write "My Family" and the child's name on each paper. Then display the family pictures on a wall at the children's eye level.

Extension: With the children, count the number of people in each Circle Family and compare the number of adults to the number of children. Then compare the sizes of the different families.

Moon Book

Make moon shapes by cutting 8-inch circles out of white construction paper. At group time, talk with your children about the round shape of the moon. Ask them to name other things they know about or can see that are round (a button, a clock, a plate, etc.). Then hold up a moon shape for each child and ask him or her to complete this sentence: "The moon reminds me of a _____." Use a felt-tip marker to sketch details on the shape according to the child's response (if the child says "a wheel," draw spokes; if the child says "a pizza," draw pepperoni circles; etc.). Let the children color their shapes with crayons. Then have them glue their shapes on sheets of construction paper and add any other details they wish. At the bottom of each paper, write the child's name and the name of the round object that he or she created ("a wheel," "a penny," etc.). Then fasten the papers together to make a book. On the cover write "The Moon Reminds Me of..." and glue on one of the white moon shapes.

Circle Story Book

Cut interesting full-page pictures out of magazines. Mount the pictures by gluing them on sheets of construction paper or inserting them in clear-plastic page protectors. Make a book by adding a construction-paper cover and fastening the pages together. Complete the book by placing a self-stick circle on each page. Show the book to your children. Ask them to find the circle on each page. Encourage them to make up stories about what the circle is doing in each picture.

Circle Hummer

Cut the rim off a round plastic lid. Use a nail to punch two holes, 1 inch apart, in the center of the circle. Thread a 16-inch piece of string through the holes and tie the ends together. Give a child the Circle Hummer. Show the child how to "wind up" the circle by moving the strings in a circular motion. Then have the child pull the string tight to make the circle hum.

Looking for Circles

Set out several round magnifying glasses. Show them to your children. Point out the circle shapes. Let the children use the magnifying glasses to search for circles in your room. You may wish to draw circles on index cards and place them around the room for the children to find.

Circle Path

Use self-stick circles to create a path on the floor. Have the children follow the path using different kinds of walks or crawls. For example, have them follow the path walking sideways, crawling backward, or jumping. If desired, have the path end at a particular place such as the door or the snack table. Or have sticker surprises waiting at the end of the path.

Hula-Hoop Games

Bring in a Hula Hoop and place it in the center of the floor. Have the children take turns walking around the outside of the hoop, heel to toe, without touching it. Then let them try jumping in and out of the Hula Hoop, walking around it with one foot inside and one foot outside, etc. Your may wish to demonstrate how to spin the Hula Hoop around your waist, and let the children try spinning it, too.

Paper-Plate Toss

Give the children small paper plates. Place a box or a laundry basket in the center of the room. Show the children how to toss their paper plates so that they sail through the air. Then let them try tossing their plates into the box or the laundry basket.

Variation: Instead of tossing paper plates into a basket, toss poker chips onto a blanket.

Circle Target

Paint a traditional circular target (a bull's-eye) on a large piece of cardboard. Attach the target to a fence or other support outdoors. Let the children take turns throwing a ball or a beanbag at the target.

This Is a Circle

Sung to: "Frere Jacques"

This is a circle, this is a circle.
How can you tell? How can you tell?
It goes round and round,
No end can be found.
It's a circle, it's a circle.

Jeanne Petty

My Favorite Shape Is a Circle

Sung to: "My Bonnie Lies Over the Ocean"

My favorite shape is a circle,
Because it's as round as can be.
The world is just full of these circles,
So think hard and name one for me.
Snowpal, snowpal,
The snowpal's a circle or two or three.
Snowpal, snowpal,
The snowpal's a circle, you see.

My favorite shape is a circle,
Because it's as round as can be.
The world is just full of these circles,
So think hard and name one for me.
Pizza, pizza,
The pizza's a circle you eat, you eat.
Pizza, pizza,
The pizza's a circle you eat.

Barbara Dunn

See the Little Circle

Sung to: "Sing a Song of Sixpence"

See the little circle

On the wall so bright,
> *(Darken room and shine a
> flashlight on a wall.)*

When I shine my flashlight

It lights up the night.

I can make my circle,

Oh, so very small,
> *(Hold flashlight close to wall
> to make small circle.)*

And I can make my circle

Grow so very, very tall.
> *(Move flashlight away from wall
> to make it grow tall.)*

Gayle Bittinger

I Can Make a Circle

Sung to: "Row, Row, Row Your Boat"

Teeny, tiny circle,

Round, as you can see.

I can make a circle,

As tiny as can be.
> *(Hold thumb and forefinger in circle shape.)*

Great, big, giant circle,

Round, as you can see.

I can make a circle,

As giant as can be.
> *(Hold arms in circle shape.)*

Gayle Bittinger

Circle Pancakes

Make pancakes using a favorite recipe. Or mix together 2 cups flour and a pinch of salt. Add 2 well-beaten eggs and just enough milk to make a thin batter. Drop the batter by spoonfuls into a hot greased skillet and cook on both sides until golden brown. Make circle-shaped pancakes in various sizes. Serve warm with butter and syrup.

Snack Wheel

Make a snack wheel by placing round crackers, carrot and cucumber rounds, and circles cut out of cheese slices on a lazy Susan. Give each of your children a round paper plate. Let the children spin the Snack Wheel around and choose snacks to put on their plates.

Fun With Squares

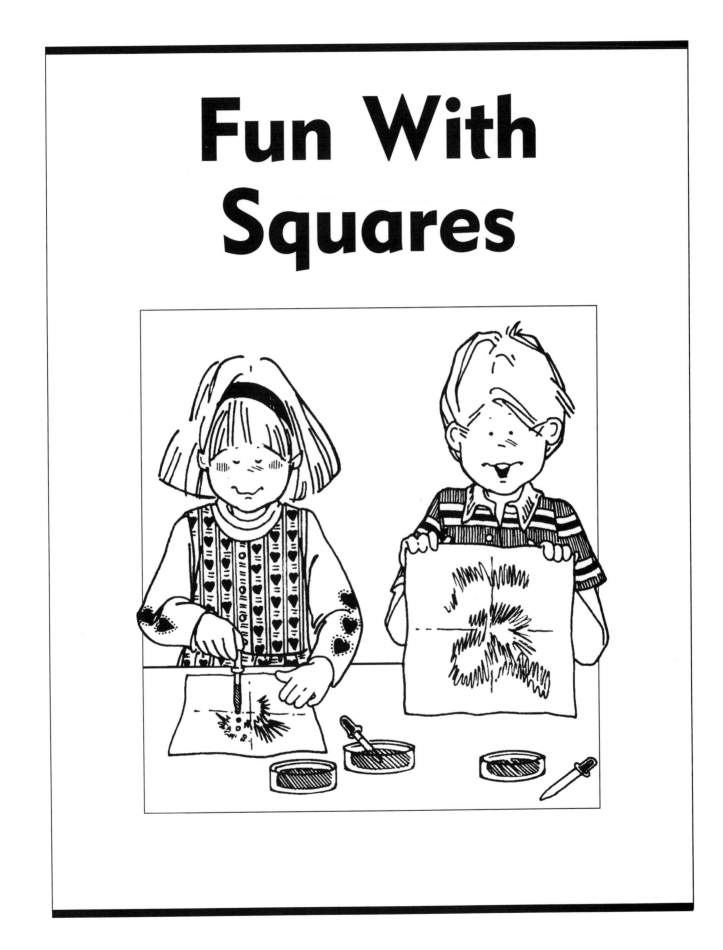

What's in the Package?

Cut wrapping paper into large squares. Hang a long piece of butcher paper at your children's eye level. Set out the wrapping-paper squares, bows, and glue. Let each child select a square and a bow. Help the children glue their bows to their squares to create packages. Then tape the top edge of each child's square package to the butcher paper, making sure no squares overlap. Then let the children look through magazines to find pictures of items they would like to have in their packages. Have them glue the pictures to the butcher paper behind their packages. Let them take turns lifting up their packages to show one another what's inside.

Square Pictures

Cut different sizes of squares out of a variety of kinds of paper such as construction paper, wrapping paper, tissue paper, and newspaper. Put the paper squares into a square box. Give each of your children a piece of construction paper cut into a square. Let the children select squares from the box to arrange and glue on their construction-paper squares.

Square Prints

Collect a variety of sizes of square blocks. Make paint pads by folding paper towels, placing them in shallow containers, and pouring on small amounts of tempera paint. Cut construction paper into square shapes. Set out all the materials. Let your children dip the blocks into the paint, then press them on the construction-paper squares to make Square Prints.

Squared-Off

Use masking tape to make several 9-inch squares on a tabletop and put a small amount of finger paint in the middle of each one. Invite one of your children to sit in front of each square and finger-paint. Encourage the children to use their fingers to trace around the edges of their squares. When the children are finished fingerpainting, show them how to use construction-paper squares to make prints of their designs.

Berry-Basket Printing

Set out plastic berry baskets and shallow containers filled with paint. Give each of your children a square piece of paper. Show the children one of the berry baskets. Have them point out the squares in the baskets. Encourage them to find small and big squares. Then let the children dip the baskets into the paint and press them on their papers to make square prints.

Designs in a Square

Find an old square baking pan and cut paper to fit inside it. Pour three colors of tempera paint into small cups. Place a marble and a spoon in each cup. Set out the materials. Have one child at a time select a piece of paper and put it in the square pan. Spoon out each marble into the pan. Let the child move the pan to make the marbles roll around. Encourage them to make the marbles roll along the edges of the pan. When the child is finished, take out his or her paper and hang it up to dry.

Craft Squares

Set out craft sticks and colored glue. Have each of your children select four craft sticks. Show the children how to glue their craft sticks together to make a square. Then let them decorate their squares with the colored glue. Tie a piece of yarn to each square and hang it up.

Variation: Instead of decorating the squares with colored glue, let your children use felt-tip markers, crayons, or paint.

Frame-Up

Provide each of your children with a square frame cut out of heavy paper. Have the children decorate their frames with crayons or felt-tip markers. Then let each child select a special piece of art. Help the children tape their artwork to the backs of their frames and hang them on the wall.

Napkin Decorating

Put several colors of thin tempera paint or food coloring into separate bowls. Set out the bowls of paint and some eyedroppers. Give each of your children a square white paper napkin. Have the children use the eye droppers to drop paint on their napkins. Encourage them to watch the colors run together. Talk about how the colors blend. Have the children unfold their napkins to discover more designs on an even larger square.

Four Corners

Out of felt, cut a large square, four small squares, four small circles, and four small triangles. Place the large square on a flannelboard and show it to your children. Point out the four equal sides and four corners of the square. Have the children count the sides and corners. Then set out the small shapes. Help the children notice the differences between the shapes. Then let the children help you place one of the small squares on each corner of the large square.

Square Outline

Draw a square on a piece of heavy paper. Set out the paper and a shoelace or a piece of thick yarn long enough to outline the square. Give the paper and shoelace or yarn to one of your children. Have the child trace over the square shape with a finger. Then let the child outline the square by placing the shoelace or yarn along the edges of the shape.

Variation: For older children, draw various sizes of squares on the heavy paper. Set out a shoelace or a piece of yarn that is just the right size for outlining each square. Let your children take turns finding which shoelace outlines which square.

Teaching Square

Cut a 12-inch square out of cardboard. Divide the square into four smaller square sections. Color each section a different color. Color four pairs of spring-type clothespins to match. Let your children take turns clipping the clothespins to the matching colored sections of the square.

Sizing Squares

Cut a small, a medium-sized, and a large house shape out of felt. Use felt-tip markers to draw doors and roofs as desired. Cut small, medium-sized, and large square window shapes out of felt. Arrange the house shapes on a flannelboard. Set out the flannelboard and the felt windows. Let each of your children select one of the windows, decide if it is small, medium-sized, or large, and place it on the matching house. Continue until all the windows are on the houses.

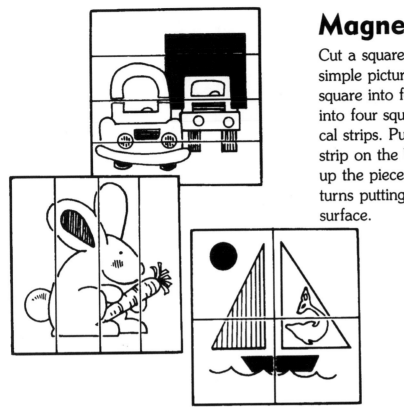

Magnetic Square Puzzle

Cut a square out of heavy paper. Draw a simple picture on the square. Divide the square into four puzzle pieces by cutting it into four squares or four horizontal or vertical strips. Put a short length of magnetic strip on the back of each puzzle piece. Mix up the pieces and let your children take turns putting the puzzle together on a metal surface.

Sorting Sponges

Find three large square sponges in different colors. Cut each large square into four smaller squares. Mix up the sponge pieces and give them to a child. Have the child sort the sponge pieces by color. Encourage the child to put the pieces back together to make three large squares.

Paper Square Fold

Give each of your children a square of plain paper. Ask your children to fold their papers in half. Then show them how to fold their papers in half again to create four smaller squares, as shown in the illustration. Have the children open their papers and let them attach a different sticker in each square.

Variation: Instead of plain paper, use graph paper. Point out the squares on the paper before folding it.

Checkerboard Fun

Set out a checkerboard and paper squares that are smaller than the squares on the board. Show your children the checkerboard. Ask them to name the shape they see over and over on it. Pass out a paper square to each child. Have the children take turns placing their paper squares on any of the squares on the checkerboard. Then remove the squares and have them put their squares on any red square, then on any black square.

Sally the Square

Cut one large square, four small squares, two 4-inch strips, and two 6-inch strips out of construction paper. Fold the strips accordion-style. Glue the shorter strips to the large square for arms and the longer ones for legs. Attach the small squares to the ends of the paper strips for hands and feet. Draw a face on the large square. Glue to a craft stick to complete the puppet. Use Sally the Square to introduce squares to your children. Have them find all the squares on Sally and tell her about all the square things they can see. Then use the puppet with the rhyme on the following page.

Animal Square Puppets

Have your children glue construction-paper squares to craft sticks. Let them use felt-tip markers, construction-paper scraps, fabric scraps, ribbon, and yarn to create animal faces on their squares. Let them use their Animal Square Puppets to talk with one another and to act out the rhyme on the following page.

Going to the Fair

Use the Sally the Square puppet (page 37) to recite the rhyme below. Have your children hold up their Animal Square Puppets (page 37). Ask the children to name the kinds of animal puppets they have made. Substitute the names of those animals for the animal names in the following rhyme.

When Sally the Square
Went to the fair,
She was all alone and blue.
Then she found a square cat
To be her friend,
And now the squares are two.

When Sally the Square
Went to the fair,
She was all alone, you see.
But she found a square cat
And then a square pig,
And now the squares are three.

When Sally the Square
Went to the fair,
She wanted to see more.
She found a square cat,
A square pig, then a duck,
And now the squares are four.

Jean Woods

This Square

Cut a large square out of yellow construction paper, a small square out of blue construction paper, and a medium-sized square out of red construction paper. Use felt-tip markers to add stripes to one square, dots to another, and wavy lines to a third. Display the squares for your children to see. Describe one of the squares and have them point to the one you are referring to. For example, you could offer descriptions such as these: "This square is the largest. This square is the color of the sun. This square has polka dots."

Blanket Rhyme

Find a blanket made of quilt squares. Show the blanket to your children while you recite the rhyme below.

I have a little blanket
Of different-colored squares.
It is my favorite blanket,
I hope it never tears.

When I go to bed,
I dream about my squares.
Sometimes they are presents,
Sometimes they are stairs.

What a lucky child I am,
I know that someone cares.
My grandma made it for me,
My blanket filled with squares.

Jean Warren

I Have Four Sides

Hold up a construction-paper square while you recite the following riddle.

I come in many sizes,
You can find me everywhere.
I have four sides, they're all the same.
Do you know what shape I am?
A square!

Kathy McCullough

Square Display

Display three square items such as a square baking pan, a square beanbag, and a square book. Ask your children to look carefully at the objects. Then have them tell you how the objects are alike and how they are different.

Is It a Square?

Out of construction paper, cut six 6-inch squares, three 6-by-3-inch rectangles, and three 9-by-6-inch rectangles. Find a 6-inch ruler or make one out of heavy paper. Set out the shapes and ruler. Explain to your children that squares have sides that are all the same length. Show them the shapes and the ruler. Ask them to use the ruler to measure the sides of each shape. Have them put the shapes with equal sides in one pile and the shapes without equal sides in another pile.

Square Shape Walk

Cut at least one square for each child and a variety of other shapes out of various colors of construction paper. Mix up the shapes and tape them to the floor. Then play music and let your children walk, skip, hop, gallop, etc., around the room. When you stop the music, have each child find a square to stand on. Ask each child to name the color of his or her square. Continue the game as long as interest lasts.

Hint: Cover the shapes with clear self-stick paper for durability, if desired.

Square Bodies

Divide your children into groups of four. Have each group try to make a square with their bodies by lying on the floor. Then have each group divide into two pairs. Ask each pair of children to figure out how to make a square with only two bodies. (Bend in half.) Finally, challenge the children to make a gigantic square with all of their bodies.

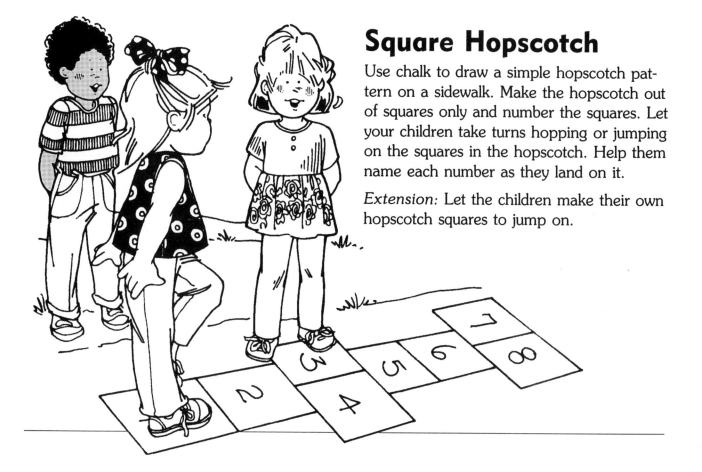

Square Hopscotch

Use chalk to draw a simple hopscotch pattern on a sidewalk. Make the hopscotch out of squares only and number the squares. Let your children take turns hopping or jumping on the squares in the hopscotch. Help them name each number as they land on it.

Extension: Let the children make their own hopscotch squares to jump on.

Floor Squares

Use masking tape to mark a large square shape on the floor. Let your children take turns walking, skipping, or crawling on the square outline. Or have the children place blocks or other objects on the tape to create a large three-dimensional shape.

This Is a Square

Sung to: "Frere Jacques"

This is a square, this is a square.
How can you tell? How can you tell?
It has four sides,
All the same size.
It's a square, it's a square.

Jeanne Petty

Squares

Sung to: "London Bridge"

Squares have four equal sides,
Equal sides, equal sides.
Squares have four equal sides,
One, two, three, four.
　　(Draw square in air with finger.)

Barbara Conahan

What Is a Square?

Sung to: "Twinkle, Twinkle, Little Star"

What is a square? Now you decide,
It has four sides, all the same size.
One side goes up, one side goes down,
One side's on top, one's on the ground.
What is a square? Now you decide,
It has four sides, all the same size.

Diane Thom

The Square Song

Sung to: "You Are My Sunshine"

I am a square, a lovely square,
I have four sides, they're all the same.
I have four corners, four lovely corners,
I am a square, that is my name.

Rita Galloway

Square Sandwiches

Cut slices of cheese, cold cuts, tomatoes, and bread into squares of the same size. Set out butter or margarine, plastic knives, and paper plates. Let your children put the square sandwich makings of their choice on their plates. Help them spread butter on their bread slices. Then let them put their Square Sandwiches together.

Crispy Square Treats

- 3 tablespoons natural-style peanut butter
- 4 to 6 tablespoons honey or pure maple syrup
- 1 cup chopped dates, raisins, or currants
- ½ cup sunflower seeds
- 2 cups crispy rice cereal

Grease an 8-inch-square baking pan. Place all the ingredients in a large bowl. Mix well with your hands. Press the mixture into the greased pan and freeze. Cut into 16 squares. Give each of your children a square. If desired, show the children how to cut each of their larger squares into four smaller squares.

Fun With Triangles

Triangle Tree Mural

Cut several large sponges into triangles and set out a piece of butcher paper. Let your children dip the sponge shapes into green tempera paint and press them all over the butcher paper to make a forest of "triangle trees." When the paint has dried, hang the paper on a wall at the children's eye level. Cut pictures of forest animals out of magazines. Let the children glue the pictures around the trees in the mural.

Cutting Triangles

Cut triangles out of various kinds of paper. Set out the triangles and some scissors. Show your children how to cut off the corners of the triangles to make little triangles. Let them cut as many triangles as they wish.

Extension: Let the children glue the triangles they cut onto large construction-paper triangles.

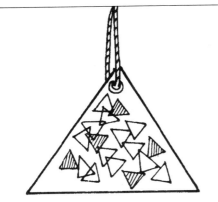

Triangle Tissue Art

Cut small triangles out of different colors of tissue paper. Set out brushes and diluted glue. Cut waxed paper into large triangle shapes. Give each child a waxed-paper triangle. Have the children brush the glue on the waxed paper and place the triangles on top of the glue. Encourage them to work on small areas at a time and to overlap their triangles to create new colors. For a shiny effect, brush more glue over the children's papers when they have finished. Allow the glue to dry. Punch a hole at the top of each triangle, attach a loop of yarn, and hang from the ceiling.

Three-Cornered Hats

For each of your children, cut a piece of 9-by-12-inch construction paper into three 9-by-4-inch strips. Cut sponges into small triangles. Pour small amounts of paint into shallow containers. Give each child three of the 9-by-4-inch strips. Let the children dip the sponges into the paint then onto their paper strips to make triangle prints. Allow the paint to dry. To complete each child's hat, staple the short ends of his or her strips together as shown in the illustration.

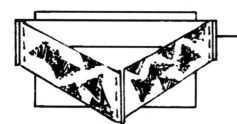

Triangle Tree

Cut 9-by-9-by-9-inch triangles out of green construction paper. (You will need a total of 4, 9, or 16 triangles to complete a tree.) Hang butcher paper on a wall or a bulletin board. Give each of your children a triangle. Let them decorate their triangles with felt-tip markers or crayons. If desired, encourage them to make triangle shapes with their markers or crayons. To make the tree, attach the decorated triangles to the butcher paper in a tree shape (see illustration). Add a brown construction-paper trunk shape to complete the tree.

Triangle Necklaces

Cut small triangles out of heavy paper and punch a hole near the top of each one. Set out the triangles and felt-tip markers. Have each of your children select several triangles to decorate with the markers. Let the children lace their decorated triangles on pieces of yarn to make Triangle Necklaces.

Sailing Art

Show the children a picture of sailboats with triangular sails. Ask them to notice the shape of the sails and the bright colors and patterns on them. Cut triangular sail shapes out of white construction paper. Give each child one of the sail shapes and a piece of construction paper with a boat and mast drawn on it. Let the children decorate their sails as they wish with felt-tip markers or crayons. Have them glue their sail shapes to the masts on their boats to complete their pictures.

Sandy Triangles

Cut triangles out of heavy paper. Set out the triangles, glue, brushes, and sand. Have your children use the brushes to spread glue all over the triangles. Encourage them to brush along the edges of the triangles before completely covering the shapes. Then let them sprinkle sand on their triangles and shake off the excess to make Sandy Triangles.

Variation: Color the sand with food coloring and let your children select the color or colors they would like to use on their triangles.

Pumpkin Faces

Cut sponges into triangular shapes of varying sizes. Pour small amounts of black paint into shallow containers. Give each of your children a pumpkin shape cut out of orange construction paper. Let the children use the triangular sponges to print faces on their pumpkin shapes.

Three Sides

Give each of your children three strips of paper and a piece of plain paper. Have the children count their strips. Show them a picture of a triangle. Help them arrange their paper strips on their papers to make a triangle. Then let them glue their strips in place on their papers. Have extra paper strips available for the children to make additional triangles if they wish.

Triangle Matching Game

Cut two triangles out of each of several patterns of wrapping paper. Make the triangles more durable by gluing them to heavy paper or covering them with clear self-stick paper. Place one triangle from each pair on a table. Give the remaining triangles to one of your children. Let the child place each of those triangles next to the matching triangle on the table.

Sail Away

Cut five simple sailboat shapes and five triangular sail shapes out of felt. Number the boats with numerals from 1 to 5. Number the sails from 1 to 5 with sets of dots. Arrange the sailboat shapes on a flannelboard. Set out the sails. Let your children take turns selecting a sail, counting the dots, and placing it above the appropriate boat on the flannelboard.

Add-a-Stroke

On a separate piece of paper for each of your children, draw several triangles, leaving off one side of each triangle. Give the papers to the children and let them complete the shapes by drawing lines with crayons or felt-tip markers.

Dot-to-Dot

For each of your children, draw dots to outline two or three different sizes of triangles on a piece of paper. Give the papers to the children. Show them how to use a crayon or felt-tip marker to connect the dots to complete their triangles. Let them decorate their triangles as desired.

Making Triangles

Provide the children with square scarves or square pieces of fabric. Demonstrate how to fold one of the scarves in half diagonally to form a triangle. Allow the children to experiment with folding the square scarves into triangles of their own. Help them discover how to keep folding their scarves into smaller and smaller triangles.

Triangle Matching

Cut four different sizes and types of triangles out of heavy paper. Place the triangles on a large piece of paper and trace around them. Mix up the triangles. Let your children take turns placing the paper triangles on the appropriate tracings.

Concentration Game

Select several small index cards and draw a triangle on each of them. Divide the cards into pairs. Color each pair of the triangles a different color. Mix up the cards and spread them out face down on a table. Let one child begin by turning up two cards. If the colors match, let the child keep the cards. If the colors don't match, have the child replace both cards face down exactly where they were before. Continue the game until all the cards have been matched. Let the children play the game as many times as they wish.

Felt Triangle Puppet

Cut two large triangles out of felt. Sew the triangles together along two sides, leaving a 2-inch finger hole in the middle of each side. Cut a small triangle out of a contrasting color of felt for the puppet's face. Add facial features cut from felt. Use the triangle puppet to introduce triangles to your children. Encourage the children to talk with the puppet about the triangles they see.

Triangle Animal Puppets

Cut triangles out of heavy paper. Decorate each triangle to look like a different animal. (See illustration.) Glue each triangle to a craft stick to complete the puppet. Give the puppets to your children. Point out the triangle shape of each puppet. Then let the children use the puppets to talk to one another.

Our Favorite Ice Cream

Cut triangular ice-cream-cone shapes out of brown construction paper. Give each of your children one of the cone shapes and a piece of construction paper. Have the children glue their cone shapes near the centers of their papers. Then let them draw a scoop of their favorite ice cream on top of their cones. Complete the following sentence on the bottom of each child's paper: "_____'s favorite ice cream is _____." Let the children "read" their papers to one another.

I Can Make a Triangle

Recite the following rhyme with your children.

I can make a triangle,

Just watch and see.

It's as easy as counting

One-two-three.

(Draw triangle in the air with finger.)

Kathy McCullough

What Is a Triangle?

Cut a paper triangle to fit in the center of a coat hanger. Write "What is a triangle?" on the paper triangle. Attach the triangle to the hanger. Cut smaller triangles out of construction paper and attach a piece of yarn to the top of each one. Brainstorm with your children the names of objects shaped like triangles. Write the words on the small triangles. Hang the triangles from the hanger. Display the hanger in your room.

Variation: Instead of writing the names of triangular objects on the small paper triangles, let your children glue pictures of the objects.

Triangle Books

Make a book for each of your children by stapling six sheets of construction paper together. Write a child's name on the cover of each book and number the inside pages from 1 to 5 with numerals and dots. Cut a variety of sizes and types of triangles out of different colors of paper. Set out the triangles and some glue. Give each child his or her book. Have them glue the appropriate number of triangles to each page. When their books are completed, let the children take turns "reading" them to one another.

Sailboat Fun

Cut 5-inch triangular sail shapes out of construction paper. Punch two holes in each sail about 2 inches apart (*see illustration*). Give each of your children a sail, a plastic drinking straw, a small lump of playdough or clay, and a small plastic container or plastic-foam food tray. Let your children use these materials to make sailboats. Have them thread their straws through the holes in their sails. Show them how to put the playdough in the middle of their containers or trays and stand the straw masts and sails upright in them. When all the boats are completed, let the children float their creations in water. Encourage them to figure out ways to make their sailboats sail across the water.

Making Triangles

Have your children sit in a circle. Give a ball of yarn to one child. Have the child hold one end of the yarn and roll the ball to another child. Have that child hold the yarn and roll the ball to a third child. Have the third child roll the ball back to the first child. Have everyone look at the triangle that they made. Wind the yarn into a ball again and repeat until each child has had a turn making a triangle. Why was a triangle made each time? How did each triangle look different? How was each triangle the same?

Extension: On an index card, sketch each triangle shape your children make. Show them the cards and let them describe each one.

Triangle Tracks

On the floor, make triangles with masking tape. Have your children push small toy cars around the outline of each triangle. Ask them questions such as these: "Which triangle is the biggest? Which one is the smallest? How do the cars drive on the corners? Which triangle is the most fun to drive on? Why?"

Triangle Hop

Set out a percussion triangle instrument. Tap out a beat on the triangle while your children walk, march, dance, or hop around the room. Vary the tempo and have the children move slowly or quickly to the beat. You may wish to let your children take turns playing the triangle.

Cool and Warm Triangle

Have your children sit in a circle. Ask one of the children to close his or her eyes while you hide a paper triangle somewhere in your room. Have the child open his or her eyes and look for the triangle while the group tells the child if he or she is cool (far away from the triangle) or warm (close to the triangle). After the child finds the triangle, have him or her hide it for the next child. Continue the game as long as interest lasts.

King or Queen of Triangles

Cover a paper crown with colorful triangles. Have your children spread out and find their own space. Place the crown on one child's head and pronounce him or her the King or Queen of Triangles. Explain that the King or Queen gets to choose a movement to do while dancing to music. Play some music and have the King or Queen tell what movement to do. Have everyone do the movement until you stop the music. Then select a new King or Queen of Triangles. Continue playing the game until each child has a chance to be King or Queen.

This Is a Triangle

Sung to: "Frere Jacques"

This is a triangle, this is a triangle.
How can you tell? How can you tell?
It has three sides
That join to form three points.
It's a triangle, it's a triangle.

Jeanne Petty

Triangles

Sung to: "Jingle Bells"

Triangles, triangles,
Have three sides.
Triangles, triangles,
Have three sides.
You can draw big triangles
In the air,
    (Use both hands to draw a triangle in the air.)
It is fun to use your hands
And make them anywhere.

Barbara Conahan

One-Two-Three

Sung to: "London Bridge"

Triangles all have three sides,
Have three sides, have three sides.
Triangles all have three sides,
Count them one-two-three.

Kathy McCullough

Found a Triangle

Sung to: "Clementine"

Found a triangle,
Found a triangle,
Found a triangle with three sides.
It can't roll,
It can't bowl,
It just sits there where it lies.

Jean Warren

Three, Please

Set out a variety of small snack foods such as O-shaped cereal, raisins, pretzels, and grapes. Give each of your children a napkin folded into a triangle. Point out the shape to the children. Have them count the sides and corners of their triangular napkins. Then let each child select three of each food item to place on his or her napkin to eat.

Triangle Cracker Fun

Purchase a box of triangular crackers. Fold square napkins diagonally to make triangles. Serve each of your children several crackers on one of the napkins. Ask your children to look at the crackers and name the shape. Have them count the sides and corners of the crackers. Show them how to arrange their crackers on their napkins to create bigger triangles (see illustration). Then let them eat their large triangles, cracker by cracker.

Fun With Rectangles

Brick Building Mural

Hang a long piece of butcher paper on a wall or a
bulletin board at your children's eye level. Cut sheets of
red 9-by-12-inch construction paper into 9-by-4-inch
rectangular "bricks." Set out the bricks and several glue
sticks. Let the children take turns gluing the bricks onto
the butcher paper to create a structure such as a house,
a fort, or a wall. Encourage them to talk about what
they are making and to work together.

Box Prints

Collect the lids of small, rectangular gift boxes. Set out the lids, shallow containers with small amounts of tempera paint in them, and sheets of paper. Let your children dip the tops or the bottoms of the lids into the paint, then onto the papers to make Box Prints. Talk about the shapes of the prints. Ask them to point out the long and short sides of each rectangle. Count the sides of the rectangles with the children.

Painted Rectangles

Fill plastic squeeze bottles with different colors of tempera paint. For each of your children, cut two rectangular shapes out of white construction paper. Give each child one of the rectangles. Let the children squeeze different-colored drops of paint on the rectangles. Give each child a second rectangle. Help the children place those rectangles on top of their painted shapes and rub across them lightly. Then have each child peel apart his or her shapes to reveal two decorated rectangles.

Rectangle Art

Cut 1-by-6-inch strips out of colored paper. Show your children how to cut the strips into three or four pieces to make small rectangles. Let the children cut as many strips as they wish into rectangles. Have the children glue their rectangles on pieces of construction paper to make Rectangle Art.

Designing Postcards

Show your children some postcards. Talk about the shape of the postcards and how they are used. Then give each child a 4-by-6-inch index card to use as a postcard. Let the children decorate one side of their postcards any way they wish with felt-tip markers. On the backs of the cards, write the children's dictated messages and the names of the intended recipients. Then let the children glue on small rectangles of colored paper for stamps.

Variation: Address each child's postcard to a person who lives in the child's home and let the children attach real postage stamps. Then take the children on a walk to mail their postcards in a nearby mailbox.

Rectangle Robots

Cut various sizes of rectangles out of different colors and kinds of paper, including shiny paper and aluminum foil. Give each of your children a piece of construction paper. Set out some glue and the rectangles. Let the children arrange the rectangles on their papers to look like robots. Have them glue the rectangles in place. Let the children add additional features to their robots with felt-tip markers.

Group Flag

Cut sheets of construction paper in half to make rectangles. Purchase solid-colored stickers in the shape of rectangles (available where office supplies are sold). Set out the construction-paper rectangles and the stickers. Ask the children to tell you what shape they are. Then let them attach the stickers to their papers to make designs. Attach the decorated papers in rows to a sheet of butcher paper to form a flag. Add a strip of dark-colored construction paper for a flagpole. Display the children's Group Flag on a wall or a bulletin board.

Hint: Make your own rectangular stickers by cutting pieces of colorful self-stick paper into rectangles.

High-Rise Mural

Hang a long sheet of dark-colored butcher paper on a wall, short side up, to represent a tall building. Give each of your children a piece of light-colored construction paper. Have them look through magazines to find pictures of people doing various activities to cut or tear out. Let them glue those pictures to their papers. Help them attach their papers to the butcher paper to add windows to the building. Ask the children to describe the shape of the building and the windows and then tell what the people in each window are doing.

Book Cover Designs

On a rectangular piece of paper, write one of your children's names and the title of his or her favorite book, to make a book cover. Repeat for each child. Have the children decorate their book covers with felt-tip markers. Display the children's rectangular book covers in your book corner.

Rectangle Hunt

Using scrap paper and a paper cutter or scissors, cut out lots of rectangles of varying sizes and colors. Hide the rectangles around the room. Explain to your children that they will be going on a Rectangle Hunt. Give each child a rectangular envelope with his or her name on it. Ask the children to look around the room for paper rectangles. As each child finds a rectangle, have the child say "Rectangle," and put it into his or her envelope. Continue until most or all of the rectangles have been found. After the hunt, help the children compare the rectangles. Lead the children to discover that even though the paper shapes are different colors and sizes, they are all rectangles.

Extension: Let your children glue the paper rectangles they found to the outsides of their envelopes or onto rectangular sheets of paper.

Mailbox Game

Make a mailbox by covering the lid of a shoebox with construction paper and cutting a slit in the top. Draw a rectangle on the lid. Collect 12 envelopes. Draw a rectangle on the fronts of half the envelopes and other shapes on the remaining half. Mix up the envelopes. Let your children take turns finding the envelopes with rectangles on them and mailing them in the rectangular mailbox.

Long and Short Game

Collect long and short sizes of identical objects such as cardboard tubes, shoelaces, rulers, and blocks. Be sure to collect two long and two short of each object. Cut a rectangle out of heavy paper. Show your children the rectangle. Have them count the sides. Point out the short and long sides of the rectangle. Then set out the long and short items. Let the children sort them into groups by length. Then have them sort them by object. Let them use each group of objects to create the outline of a rectangle.

Postcard Puzzles

Collect a number of rectangular picture postcards. Cut each postcard into several pieces to make a simple puzzle. Put each postcard puzzle in a resealable plastic bag. Let your children take turns selecting a puzzle and putting it together. Point out the shape of postcard puzzle when it is completed.

Sequence Cards

To make a set of sequence cards that shows how a rectangle is drawn, place four index cards on a table. On the first card, draw one side of a rectangle. On the second card, draw two sides; on the third card, draw three sides; and on the fourth card, draw all four sides. Mix up the cards. Let your children take turns arranging the cards in sequence.

Extension: Give your children pieces of paper and crayons. Let them try drawing their own rectangles in the order shown on the cards.

Shopping for Rectangles

Collect empty food containers in a variety of shapes. Set out the containers on some shelves to make a miniature grocery store. Let your children take turns "shopping" for items that are rectangular. Have them put their items in a basket or a child-size shopping cart. Let them pay for their purchases with rectangular play money.

Extension: Find rectangular coupons to match the rectangular food containers. Let your children match the coupons to the food items.

License Plate Fun

Cut rectangles the size of license plates out of heavy paper and set them aside. Find a real license plate and show it to your children. Talk about its shape. Point out the two short sides and the two long sides. Then provide each child with one of the paper "license plates." Use glue to write each child's name on his or her license plate. Let the children sprinkle glitter over the glue to make their own personalized license plates.

I Spy a Rectangle

Have your children sit in a rectangle in the middle of the room. Let them glance around the room as you call attention to different rectangular objects. Then let one child begin, saying, "I spy a rectangle with my little eye." Have the other children try to guess what the object is. When a player guesses correctly, let him or her have the next turn.

Rectangle Books

Make a book for each of your children by stapling together four sheets of plain paper and a colored construction-paper cover. Title the book "My Rectangle Book." Let your children look through magazines and catalogs to find pictures of objects shaped like rectangles. Have them tear or cut out the pictures and glue them in their books. (Let younger children choose from precut pictures that have been placed in a box.) Let your children "read" their books to you.

Book Fun

Collect a variety of rectangular books. Show your children the books. Ask them to name the shape of each one. Then let the children pick out one or two books for you to read to them. As you are reading, encourage the children to look at the pictures to find objects shaped liked rectangles.

Knock, Knock

Have your children stand by a rectangular door and point out its shape. Then ask one child to pretend to be a trick-or-treater, stand behind the door, and knock on it. When you answer the door, say the rhyme below. Pause when you get to the blank and have the child describe what costume he or she is wearing.

Knock, knock, sounds like more
Trick-or-treaters at my door.
I open the door and what do I see?
A _____ smiling at me.

Jean Warren

Who Am I?

Hold up a rectangular picture frame with the glass and backing removed. Have one of your children stand behind the frame so his or her face shows through. Have the other children ask the child questions such as these: "What is your name? How old are you? What is your favorite game?" Repeat until each child has had a chance to stand behind the frame.

Name the Rectangle

Have your children sit in a circle. In the middle of the circle, set out a rectangular box, several items that are rectangular (video cassette, magazine, placemat, etc.), and several items that are clearly not rectangular (ball, pine cone, candle, etc.). Tell your children that you would like to put the rectangular items in the rectangular box. Ask the children to tell you which objects would go in the box, which items would not, and why.

Front and Back

Arrange rectangular carpet mats on the floor to resemble a long train. Have your children sit on the mats. Discuss who is sitting in the front of the train, who is in the middle, and who is in the back. Then have your children change places. Ask them to now tell you who is in the front, who is in the middle, and who is in back. Continue as long as interest lasts.

Hint: For a large group of children, make several smaller trains instead of one long train.

Will It Fit?

Provide each child with a rectangular
shoebox. Put out several objects that will fit
into the boxes and several that will not.
Have the children look at the objects and
predict which ones they think will fit into
their boxes. Then have them test their predictions. Help them compare their
predictions with their results.

Infinity Mirror

Set up two rectangular mirrors directly facing each other, about 3 feet apart. Let your
children take turns standing between the
mirrors to discover the multiple reflections
that are made. (Two mirrors placed face to
face create an infinity mirror, with endless
reflections.) Give each child a rectangle to
hold. How many rectangles can he or she
see in the mirrors?

Magic Rectangle

Place a rectangular rug or carpet mat in the middle of your room. Have your children form a line and choose one child to be the leader. Play some music and let the children march around the room, crossing over the Magic Rectangle as they march. Stop the music and let the child standing on the rectangle be the new leader. Start the music again. Be sure to time the music so that each child has a turn leading the line.

Musical Rectangles

Place rectangular carpet mats, one for each child, on the floor in a circle. Ask your children to tell you what shape the mats are. Then ask each child to stand on one of the mats. Begin playing some music and have the children walk around on the mats. Take away one of the mats. When you stop the music, have each child find a mat to sit on or touch in some way (with a foot, a hand, an elbow, a knee, etc.). In order to do this, at least two children will have to share a mat. Continue to start and stop the music, removing one mat each time. As the game progresses, the children will be sharing fewer and fewer mats. When you have one mat left and all the children are sharing it, the game is over.

Pillow Jump

Collect as many rectangular pillows as possible. Place the pillows in a big pile. Show the pillows to your children. Talk about the shape of the pillows. Ask them to point out big and small rectangles. Then let the children take turns piling up and jumping into the pillows.

Rectangle Walk

Use masking tape to make large outlines of several sizes of rectangles on the floor. Let your children take turns walking, crawling, marching, or hopping around the edges of the rectangles. Or ask the children to stand on the long or short edges of the rectangles.

This Is a Rectangle

Sung to: "Frere Jacques"

This is a rectangle, this is a rectangle.
How can you tell? How can you tell?
It has two short sides,
And it has two long sides.
It's a rectangle, it's a rectangle.

Jeanne Petty

Rectangles

Sung to: "Jingle Bells"

Rectangles, rectangles
Have four sides.
Two are long and two are short,
> *(Hold hands far apart, then close together.)*
Please give them a try.
> *(Draw rectangle in air with finger.)*
Rectangles, rectangles
Have four sides.
Two are long and two are short,
> *(Hold hands far apart, then close together.)*
Please give them a try.
> *(Draw rectangle in air with finger.)*

Barbara Conahan

I'm a Rectangle

Sung to: "Frere Jacques"

I'm a rectangle, I'm a rectangle,
Look at me, look at me!
I have four sides,
Two short and two long.
I'm a rectangle, I'm a rectangle.

Kathy McCullough

Find a Rectangle

Sung to: "Row, Row, Row Your Boat"

Point to a rectangle,
You'll find them all around.
A door, a book, just take a look,
Now Molly find us one.
    (Have child point to rectangle.)

Sing the song for each of your children, substituting
the name of the child for *Molly*.

Kathy McCullough

Rectangle Snack

Serve a variety of rectangular foods on a rectangular tray. Some possibilities include rectangular snack crackers, cheese or meat slices cut into rectangles, or any kind of sandwich cut into rectangles. Give your children rectangular napkins to place on rectangular placemats. Provide them with juice in rectangular boxes as well.

Cracker Rectangles

Set out whole graham crackers, peanut butter, and plastic knives. Ask your children to tell you the shape of the graham crackers. Then let each child select a graham cracker. Put some peanut butter on each graham cracker and let the children use the plastic knives to spread it around. Ask them to spread the peanut butter from short side to short side, or from long side to long side. Have them take a bite out of a long side, then one out of a short side.

Fun With Ovals

Up, Up, and Away

Cut large oval shapes out of white construction paper. Fill spray bottles with diluted tempera paint. Hang one of the oval shapes on an easel. Ask one of your children to come over to the easel and spray-paint the oval. Repeat until each child has had a chance to paint one of the ovals. Allow the paint to dry. Hang a sheet of light blue or white butcher paper on a wall or a bulletin board. Let the children attach their ovals to the paper. Use brown crayons to add baskets and ropes to the ovals to make hot-air balloons (see illustration).

Oval Placemat Art

Purchase oval-shaped vinyl placemats in plain colors. (Or cut rectangular vinyl placemats into oval shapes.) Set them out on a table. Let your children decorate the ovals with water-based felt-tip markers. Encourage them to notice the shapes of the placemats. You may wish to cut small ovals out of the placemats for the children to draw around and incorporate into their decorations. When the children are finished, wash or wipe off their designs and set out the placemats to be drawn on again.

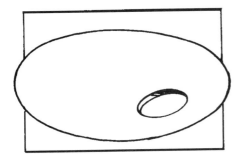

Bean Ovals

For each of your children, use a crayon to draw three different sizes of ovals on a piece of construction paper. Set out brushes, glue, and a variety of oval-shaped dried beans. Let the children brush glue on their papers, then arrange the beans in and around the ovals. Encourage older children to glue beans around the oval outlines or to create patterns with the various dried beans.

Yarn-Covered Ovals

For each of your children cut a 6-inch oval shape out of a plastic-foam food tray. Cut ½-inch slits around the edge of each oval. Cut yarn into 3-foot lengths. Tape one end of a piece of yarn to the back of each oval and pull it through one of the slits. Give each child one of the prepared ovals. Let the children wind the yarn around their ovals, each time passing the yarn through one of the slits. Encourage them to criss-cross their ovals any way they wish to create designs. When the children have finished, trim off the ends of the yarn and tape them to the backs of the ovals.

Basket of Eggs

Give each of your children a piece of light-blue construction paper with a simple basket shape drawn on it. Pour thick white and brown tempera paint into separate shallow containers. Let the children add "eggs" to their baskets by dipping one finger at a time into the paint and pressing their fingers in and around the basket shapes on their papers.

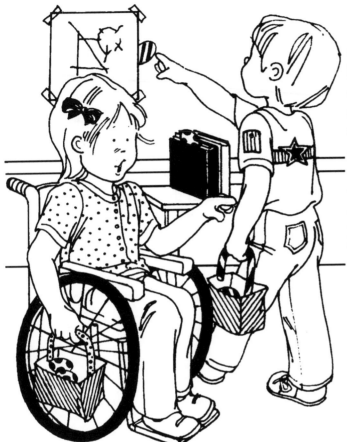

Hunting for Ovals

Cut paper lunch sacks in half and use the bottom halves to make baskets. To complete each basket, cut a handle out of a different-colored piece of construction paper or wallpaper and attach it to the sack. Then cut six small oval shapes for each basket from paper that matches the handle. Hide the ovals in various places around the room. Give each of your children one of the baskets and let them go on a hunt for ovals. When they find ovals that match their handles, have them put those ovals in their baskets. Continue until all the ovals have been found.

Egg-Carton Game

Cut 12 oval shapes and 12 other shapes out of construction paper. Mix up the shapes and put them in a basket. Set out the basket and an egg carton. Let your children take turns finding the oval shapes in the basket and putting them in the egg carton.

Texture Ovals

Cut pairs of oval shapes from a variety of textured materials such as sandpaper, flocked wallpaper, furry fabric, and felt. Place one of each pair in a box and set the rest out on a table. To play the game, let your children take turns selecting an oval shape from the table, closing their eyes, and reaching into the box to find its match.

Whose Nest?

Cut five mother-hen shapes, five nest shapes, and 15 oval egg shapes out of felt. Number the hens from 1 to 5. Glue a different number of eggs (from 1 to 5) on each nest shape. Place the nests and the mother hens on a flannelboard. Let your children help the mother hens find their nests by counting the eggs and matching each hen to the appropriate nest.

Egghead Puppet

Cut an oval egg shape out of an index card. Cut it in two pieces, making the top half slightly larger than the bottom half. Glue the top half of the egg shape to the top side of a spring-type clothespin and the bottom half to the bottom side. Draw an eye on the top half and decorate as desired. Squeeze the clothespin to make the two halves of the egg shape open and close, resembling a talking mouth. Use the Egghead Puppet to introduce oval-shaped objects to your children.

Four Colored Eggs

Cut one oval egg shape from each of the following colors of felt: blue, green, red, yellow. Place the shapes on a flannelboard as you read the poem below.

Blue egg, blue egg,
Oh, what fun!
Blue egg, blue egg,
I found one.

Green egg, green egg,
I see you.
Green egg, green egg,
Now I've two.

Red egg, red egg,
Now I see.
Red egg, red egg,
Now I've three.

Yellow egg, yellow egg,
Just one more.
Yellow egg, yellow egg,
Now I've four.

Jean Warren

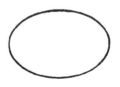

When Will It Sink?

Fill a sink or a plastic dishpan with water and float a lighweight plastic container in it. Set out a dish of large, oval-shaped beans. Ask your children to guess how many beans it will take to make the container sink into the water. Then let them carefully add one bean at a time to the container while you count. When the container sinks, have them compare the number of beans on it to the number they guessed. Let them experiment with placing the beans in different places in the container to see if they can make it sink with more or less beans.

Nests for Eggs

With your children, discuss birds and the nests they build for the eggs that they lay. Talk about how birds build their nests with twigs, leaves, and whatever else they can find. Show the children a picture of a nest with eggs in it. What shape are the eggs? Then take your children on a walk to observe birds and their nests.

Running in Ovals

Make a running track in a large indoor room or outside. Designate the track by making an oval with masking tape or by arranging chairs or plastic cones in an oval shape. Let your children run around the oval track as many times as they wish. Encourage them to think of other ways they could move around the track.

Cross the River

Cut large oval stone shapes out of gray construction paper. Designate a river by placing two long strips of masking tape on the floor about 8 feet apart. Tape the stone shapes in various places across the river. Let your children take turns crossing the river by stepping only on the stones. Encourage them to use a variety of paths to cross the river.

This Is an Oval

Sung to "Frere Jacques"

This is an oval, this is an oval.
How can you tell? How can you tell?
It's long on one end
And short on the other.
It's an oval, it's an oval.

Gayle Bittinger

Did I Fool You?

Sung to: "Up on the Housetop"

I am round, this is true,
But I just might fool you.
One way I'm thin, one way I'm tall,
If you stand me up, I'm sure to fall.
I am an oval, this is true.
I am an oval, did I fool you?
One way I'm thin, one way I'm tall,
If you stand me up, I'm sure to fall.

Gayle Bittinger

Egg-Shaped Sandwiches

Cut slices of bread into oval egg shapes and spread them with peanut butter. Then let your children decorate their Egg-Shaped Sandwiches with shredded carrots, banana slices, and raisins.

Decorated Drinking Straws

Cut small oval shapes out of construction paper. Cut a small slit in the top and bottom of each oval. Give each of your children one of the ovals and a plastic drinking straw. Have your children decorate their ovals with crayons, then stick their straws through the slits. Let your children use their straws to drink their beverage at snacktime.

Fun With Diamonds

Diamond Quilt Mural

Cut small diamond shapes out of colorful paper and aluminum foil. Give each of your children a 9-inch-square piece of construction paper. Let the children glue the small paper and foil diamonds in patterns on the squares. Arrange the squares in a quilt shape (see illustration) on the floor and tape them all together. Carefully hang the paper quilt on a wall or a bulletin board.

Sparkling Diamonds

Cut clear self-stick paper into 6- or 7-inch diamond shapes. Cut two shapes for each of your children. Remove the backing from each shape. Set out the diamond shapes and metallic paper confetti (available at card and gift stores). Give each child one of the self-stick diamond shapes. Let the children arrange some of the metallic confetti on their diamonds. As each child finishes, put a second self-stick diamond on top of his or her decorated diamond and press them together. Punch a hole in the top of each completed diamond and tie a loop of yarn through it. Hang the diamonds near a window where they will sparkle in the sunshine.

Hint: If metallic paper confetti is not available, make your own out of shiny wrapping paper and aluminum foil using scissors or a hole punch.

Diamond Crowns

Make a crown for each of your children out of construction paper. From other colors and kinds of paper, cut out small diamond shapes. Give the children their crowns and let them glue on the small diamond shapes to represent jewels.

Diamond Rubbings

Cut diamond shapes out of various textured materials such as sandpaper, corrugated cardboard, plastic needlework canvas, and corduroy fabric. Glue the shapes to a 9-by-12-inch sheet of heavy paper. Show your children how to place a piece of thin paper over the diamond shapes and rub across them with the flat side of a crayon to make a rubbing. Let your children take turns making rubbings over the diamond shapes.

Diamond Kite Pictures

Give each of your children a diamond kite shape (about 7 inches long) cut from white construction paper and folded in half lengthwise. Ask the children to name the shape. Then have them open their shapes and use eyedroppers to squeeze drops of tempera paint on one of the sides. Have them refold their papers, rub over them gently with their hands, and then open them to see the designs they created. When the paint has dried, let the children glue their diamond kite shapes, along with pieces of yarn for kite strings, on sheets of blue construction paper.

Number Cards

Find an old deck of playing cards. Take out the diamond cards from 1 to 10 and the club cards from 1 to 10. Mix up the cards. Let one of your children sort the cards into two piles. Help the child arrange the cards in each pile from 1 to 10, or have the child find the matching numbered pairs. Mix up the cards again and let another child sort and arrange them.

Diamond Match-Up

Cut large squares out of posterboard. On each square, arrange four or more craft sticks to make a different kind of diamond shape (large, small, wide, narrow, etc.). Trace around the craft sticks. Spread the squares out on the floor and set out a box of craft sticks. Let your children create matching shapes by placing craft sticks on top of the tracings on the squares.

103

Kite Puzzles

Cut 10 kite shapes out of different patterned wallpaper samples. Cover the shapes with clear self-stick paper for durability, if desired. Cut each kite shape in half lengthwise. Mix up the halves and let your children take turns putting the Kite Puzzles back together.

Dig for Diamonds

Cut diamond shapes and other shapes out of cardboard. Cover the diamond shapes with aluminum foil. Hide the diamonds and other shapes in a box of sand. Let your children take turns digging in the sand with their hands or a shovel. Have them put any diamonds they find in a bucket. Let them toss any other shapes they find back into the sand. When they are finished, have them count the number of diamonds they found.

Diamond Signs

Collect pictures of diamond-shaped traffic signs by taking photographs of signs in your neighborhood, drawing your own signs, or finding a book with pictures of traffic signs. Show your children the signs. Ask them to notice the shape of the signs. Then help them read the words or symbols on each sign. Talk about what they mean.

Extension: Take your children on a walk to look for diamond-shaped traffic signs.

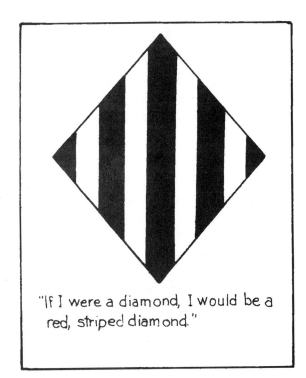

"If I were a diamond, I would be a red, striped diamond."

Diamond Book

Provide each of your children with a piece of paper with a diamond drawn on it. Have each of them complete the following sentence: "If I were a diamond, I would be a _____, _____ diamond." Write each child's sentence on his or her paper below the diamond. Let the children decorate their diamonds according to their descriptions. Staple the pages together. Read the book to the children, allowing each child to "read" his or her page to the others.

Find the Diamonds

On a sheet of paper, draw several large diamonds that overlap to make smaller diamonds (see illustration). Show the paper to your children. Ask them to look carefully at the paper and tell you how many diamonds are drawn on it. If necessary, point out the smaller diamonds made by the larger diamonds. Draw a different arrangement of diamonds on another sheet of paper and show it to the children. Ask them to count the diamonds again. Repeat as long as interest lasts.

Shiny and Dull

Show your children a picture of a real diamond. Talk about how shiny the diamond is and how it sparkles. Then show the children something that is dull such as a piece of paper or a wooden block. Ask the children to look around the room and find other shiny and dull objects. Have them compare the objects they found. How are the shiny objects alike? How are they different from the dull objects? Which one do they like best?

Extension: Have your children compare the real diamond to a diamond shape. How are they the same? How are they different? If possible, show the children pictures of different-shaped diamonds.

Baseball Diamond Fun

Set up a baseball diamond inside or outside by cutting cardboard into diamond shapes for the bases and arranging them in a diamond shape. Let your children take turns standing at home plate, pretending to hit a baseball, and running around the bases.

Extension: Take your children to a baseball or softball field and let them run the bases there.

Collect the Treasure

Cut diamond shapes out of shiny paper, four or five for each of your children. Scatter the diamonds on the floor. Tell your children that they are going to take turns collecting the diamond treasure that has been lost. Place a bucket in the center of the floor. Then give each child 30 seconds to pick up as many diamonds as he or she can, one at a time, and put them in the bucket.

Hint: Do not count the final amount or compare how many diamonds each child collected. The fun is in the doing! If you have a large group, let two children at a time collect diamonds.

This Is a Diamond

Sung to: "Frere Jacques"

This is a diamond, this is a diamond.
How can you tell? How can you tell?
It has four points,
It stands on one point.
It's a diamond, it's a diamond.

Gayle Bittinger

Found a Diamond

Sung to: "Clementine"

Found a diamond, found a diamond,
Found a diamond in the sand.
I think I'll make a necklace
With the diamond in my hand.

Continue with additional verses and let your
children name what they would make with a
diamond.

Jean Warren

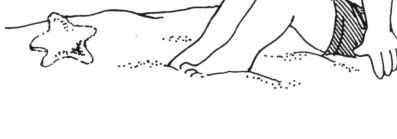

Kite Sandwiches

Cut bread and cheese slices into diamond kite shapes. Give each of your children one of the cheese shapes and two of the bread shapes on a small plate. Let the children spread butter or margarine on their bread slices, if desired. Then have them put their bread and cheese slices together to make Kite Sandwiches.

Baseball Diamond Snack

Arrange four small tables in a baseball diamond shape. Set plates or bowls at "home plate." Put a different snack food on each of the other bases. Let your children pick up their plates or bowls and walk around the bases to serve their snacks.

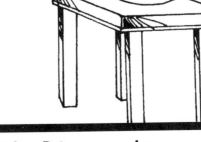

Fun With Hearts

Patchwork Heart Mural

Cut an extra-large heart shape out of butcher paper. Cut the heart into sections (one for each or your children). Mark the back side of each section with a pencil. Let the children use crayons or felt-tip markers to decorate the front sides of their sections any way they wish. When they have finished, help them put their patchwork heart together like a puzzle and glue it to a bigger piece of butcher paper. Then hang the heart on a wall or a bulletin board.

Variation: Instead of having the children decorate their sections with crayons or felt-tip markers, let them attach heart-shaped stickers.

Heart Stamping

To make a heart stamp, cut a heart shape out of a plastic-foam food tray. Cut a 1-by-4-inch strip out of cardboard. Fold the strip in half, fold up the ends, then tape the ends to the back of the plastic-foam heart to make a handle (see illustration). Make as many heart stamps as desired. Make paint pads by folding paper towels in half, placing them in shallow containers, and pouring on small amounts of paint. Set out the paint pads and heart stamps. Give each of your children a piece of paper cut into a heart shape. Let the children use the heart stamps to make designs on their heart papers.

Heart Rubbings

Set out a large square of plastic needlework canvas (available at craft stores). Cut heart shapes out of plain paper. Let your children take turns placing the heart shapes on top of the plastic lace square and rubbing across them with crayons.

Heart Stencils

Collect several plastic lids and remove the rims. Draw a different kind of heart shape in the center of each lid. Using a sharp knife, cut out each heart shape and discard, keeping the lid with the heart-shaped hole in it. Set out the lids, paint, paintbrushes, and construction paper. Show your children how to place a lid on a piece of paper, paint over the cut-out heart, and carefully lift up the lid to reveal the heart shape on the paper. Then let the children use the stencils to make various heart shapes on the construction paper.

Hearty Creatures

Cut various sizes of hearts out of different colors of construction paper. Set out glue and the construction-paper hearts. Let your children glue the hearts together any way they wish to create Hearty Creatures. Have them add details with crayons or felt-tip markers. Display the children's creations on a wall or a bulletin board.

Heart Halves

For each of your children, cut several heart shapes from different colors of construction paper. Show your children how to cut their hearts in half. Hand out large pieces of white paper and glue. Have the children find the two halves of each of their paper hearts. Then have them put their heart halves together and glue them on their papers to create whole hearts.

Hearts for Counting

From light-colored construction paper, cut out five heart shapes (or tear pages from a heart-shaped note pad). Use a felt-tip marker to number the shapes from 1 to 5. Cover the shapes with clear self-stick paper. Set out a small rubber stamp in the shape of a heart and a dark-colored washable ink pad. Let your children take turns identifying the numerals on the hearts and stamping on the corresponding numbers of heart prints. As each child finishes, wipe the ink off the shapes with a damp paper towel.

Heart Puzzle

Select a heart-shaped, non-aluminum pan. Cut a piece of heavy paper to fit inside the pan. Cut the paper into several puzzle pieces. Put a piece of magnetic strip on the back of each puzzle piece. Give one of your children the pan and the puzzle pieces. Let the child put the puzzle back together in the pan.

Variation: Use a heart-shaped candy box and puzzle pieces without magnetic strips.

Heart Patterns

Collect several different kinds of heart stickers. For each of your children, put three or four different stickers on a piece of paper in a row to make a pattern. Then give the children more stickers and let them continue the patterns on their papers.

Variation: Instead of stickers, cut small heart shapes out of various colors of construction paper and glue them to the papers.

Heart Book

Cut construction paper into identical, large heart shapes. Ask your children to think about people they love. Have each child dictate an ending for this sentence: "I love _____." Print each child's completed sentence on one of the heart-shaped pages and let the child add an illustration with crayons or felt-tip markers. Cover the pages with clear self-stick paper. Then fasten them together by punching holes in the upper left-hand corners and inserting a metal ring or a loop of yarn. Let the children "read" their pages to one another before placing the Heart Book in the book corner.

Heart Tree

Stand a tree branch in a pot of soil. Ask your children to name ways they can show love or kindness to others such as helping to put away toys, setting the table, or sharing crayons with friends. Then have each child dictate a sentence to you telling how he or she will show love or kindness to someone else. Print each child's sentence on a separate construction-paper heart shape. Hang the hearts on the tree branch with string or yarn to create a Heart Tree.

Mirror Hearts

Cut small heart shapes from construction paper. Then cut the hearts in half. Give each of your children a hand mirror and half of a paper heart. Have the children place their heart halves on a table. Let them experiment with standing their hand mirrors next to their heart halves to make the half-hearts appear to be whole hearts.

Hearts for the Birds

Let each of your children use a heart-shaped cookie cutter to cut a heart shape out of a slice of stale bread. Have the children spread peanut butter on their hearts and then sprinkle on birdseed. Insert a pipe cleaner through each heart to make a hanger. Help the children hang their hearts on a tree outside a window in your room. Let them also spread the leftover bread pieces on the ground around the tree. Encourage the children to watch for the birds that come to enjoy their special heart treats.

Heart Number Hop

For each of your children, cut a large heart shape out of construction paper. Write a familiar numeral on each of the hearts, repeating numerals if necessary. Have the children sit in a circle. Place a heart face down in front of each child. To start the game, stand behind a child. Have that child pick up his or her heart, identify the number on it, and place it back on the floor. Then, while you sit down in the child's place, have him or her hop that number of times from child to child to find out who gets to take the next turn. Continue playing until each child has had a chance to do a Heart Number Hop.

Mending Broken Hearts

For every two children, cut one heart shape out of red posterboard. Draw a jagged line down the center of each heart and cut along the line to make two puzzle pieces. (Make sure that the pieces of each heart fit together differently.) Give each of your children a heart half. Let the children search for the matching halves of their hearts and fit them together. Congratulate each pair of children when they have sucessfully "mended their broken heart."

This Is a Heart

Sung to: "Frere Jacques"

This is a heart, this is a heart.
How can you tell? How can you tell?
It's rounded on the top
And pointy at the bottom.
It's a heart, it's a heart.

Gayle Bittinger

Here's a Heart

Sung to: "London Bridge"

Here's a heart that's colored red,
Colored red, colored red.
Here's a heart that's colored red
"Show me first," it said.

Here's a heart that's colored blue,
Colored blue, colored blue.
Here's a heart that's colored blue,
I made it just for you.

Here's a heart that's colored green,
Colored green, colored green.
Here's a heart that's colored green,
The prettiest that I've seen.

Additional verses: Here's a heart that's colored
white, It's a beautiful sight; Here's a heart that's
colored brown, It's the best in town; Here's a heart
that's colored black, On its front and back; Here's a
heart that's colored pink, And that's the end, I think.

Hold up matching colored paper hearts as they are
named in the song.

Gayle Bittinger

Heart Waffles

Toast frozen waffles and let your children use heart-shaped cookie cutters to cut them into heart shapes. Then let the children decorate their waffle hearts by sprinkling on powdered sugar.

Hearty Bear Sandwiches

Have your children use heart-shaped cookie cutters to cut heart shapes out of whole-wheat bread slices (partially frozen bread cuts more easily). Show them how to cut off the points of their hearts to make the bread resemble bear faces. Then let each child spread peanut butter on his or her bear face and use raisins to make eyes and a mouth and a red grape to make a nose.

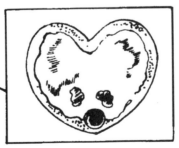

Fun With Stars

Stars in the Night Sky

Cut 6-inch star shapes out of cardboard. Tear aluminum foil into 12-inch sheets. Hang dark blue or black butcher paper on a wall or a bulletin board at your children's eye level. Set out the star shapes and sheets of foil. Let the children carefully wrap the foil around the stars. Help them attach their foil-covered stars to the butcher paper. Add a yellow construction-paper moon shape to complete the night-sky scene.

To Make a Star

Fold a rectangular piece of paper in half. Then, with the folded edge at the bottom, fold the paper as indicated by the arrows and dotted lines in the illustration below. Cut through all thicknesses as shown. Make several stars for each of your children. Let them decorate their stars as they wish.

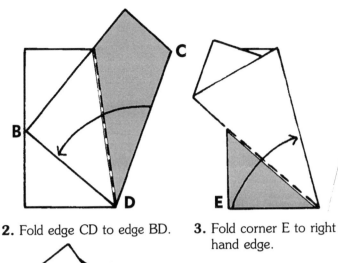

2. Fold edge CD to edge BD.

3. Fold corner E to right hand edge.

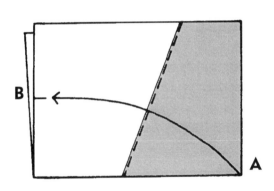

1. Fold corner A to midpoint B on left edge.

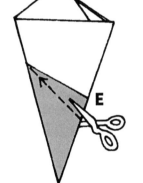

4. Cut through all layers about one quarter down from line E.

5. Unfold.

6.

Star Sticker Fun

Purchase a package of self-stick stars (available at office supply stores). Cut large star shapes out of construction paper. Let your children decorate their star shapes with the star stickers. As each page of stickers is used up, set out the empty sticker sheets and thin paper. Let your children place the sticker sheets under the thin paper to make star rubbings.

Star Prints

Make a paste out of flour and water and pour small amounts of it into shallow containers. Collect several star-shaped cookie cutters. Set out the paste, cookie cutters, pieces of dark-colored construction paper, and glitter or salt. Have your children dip the cookie cutters into the paste mixture and then press them onto the pieces of construction paper to make prints. Show them how to carefully sprinkle a little glitter or salt over their sticky stars and shake off any excess into a big box to use again. Let the children make as many Star Prints as they wish.

Star Surprises

For each of your children, use a white crayon to draw stars on a piece of white construction paper. (Press down hard with the crayon while drawing.) Set out the papers along with brushes and black tempera paint thinned with water to make a wash. Then let the children brush the tempera wash over their papers to discover the Star Surprises that will show through.

Counting-Card Packs

For each of your children, number five index cards from 1 to 5. Set out ink pads and small star-shaped rubber stamps. Let your children stamp corresponding numbers of prints on their numbered cards. Give the children envelopes or resealable plastic bags for storing their individual card packs. Encourage them to exchange packs with friends and count one anothers' designs. Or have them find matching numbered cards in both of their packs.

Variation: Instead of using star-shaped rubber stamps, let your children attach self-stick stars.

Search for Your Star

Cut star shapes out of heavy paper. Write one of your children's name on each star. Hang the stars around the room. Have the children search for their stars while they "wonder where they are." When each child has found his or her star, recite or sing "Twinkle, Twinkle, Little Star" together.

Sizing Up Stars

Cut several sizes of stars out of various colors of construction paper. Cover the stars with clear self-stick paper for durability, if desired. Let your children sort them according to the sizes of small, medium, and large. Have them count the stars in each pile. Then help them count all the stars together. Finally, select several different sizes of stars and have the children arrange them in order from smallest to largest.

Star Colors Game

Cut a star out of heavy paper and color each of its five points a different color. Then color the ends of five spring-type clothespins to match the colors on the star points. To play the game, let your children take turns clipping each clothespin on the matching star point.

Wish Upon a Star

Cut a star shape out of cardboard and cover it with foil. Tell your children that it is a special wishing star and that whoever holds it gets to make a wish. Then give the star to one child and let him or her make a wish. Pass the star around the group until everyone has had a turn making a wish.

Four Little Stars

Cut four star shapes out of felt. Place the stars on a flannelboard. As you recite the following poem, remove the stars one at a time.

Four little stars winking at me,
One shot off, then there were three.

Three little stars with nothing to do,
One shot off, then there were two.

Two little stars afraid of the sun,
One shot off, then there was one.

One little star not having any fun,
It shot off, then there were none.

Jean Warren

Constellations

Explain to your children that a constellation is a group of stars in the sky that has a certain shape and a name. The Big Dipper (Ursa Major) is a constellation that looks like a ladle. Other constellations look like a swan, a bear, a fish, etc. If possible, show the children some pictures of constellations. Then set out black construction paper and self-stick stars. Let the children use the stars to create their own constellations on the black paper. Encourage them to name their constellations as well.

Sea-Star Fun

Show your children a picture of a sea star or, if possible, a real sea star. Talk about the shape of the sea star and count its arms. Tell them that each arm has tube feet with suction disks at the ends. A sea star uses the suction disks for crawling and attaching to hard surfaces. Give each child a plastic suction cup (cut from an old bath mat or the kind used to hang ornaments on a window). Show them how the suction cups stick to smooth surfaces. Then let the children pretend to be sea stars and use their suction cups to crawl and attach to smooth surfaces in the room.

Reach for the Stars

Use yarn to hang paper stars from the ceiling at different levels. Hang the lowest stars so that they can easily be touched by all your children. Hang the highest stars so that the children will have to jump to touch them. Then let the children take turns jumping and reaching for the stars!

The Sea-Star Walk

Divide your children into groups of five. Have each group stand in a circle with their backs together. Have them hold their arms out in front of them and hold hands with one another. Let the groups move like sea stars from "rock to rock" around the room.

This Is a Star

Sung to: "Frere Jacques"

This is a star, this is a star.
How can you tell? How can you tell?
It has five points
Coming from the center.
It's a star, it's a star.

Gayle Bittinger

Star Stomp

Sung to: "Hokey-Pokey"

You do the Star Stomp here,
You do the Star Stomp there,
You do the Star Stomp here,
Now you do it everywhere.
Just stomp right on the stars
That you find on the floor,
Then stomp just a little more.

Tape small paper stars on the floor. While you sing the song, have your children stomp on all the stars they can find.

Gayle Bittinger

Star Snacks

Serve your children slices of star fruit on paper plates cut into star shapes. Or serve star-shaped crackers. Or use small, star-shaped cookie cutters to cut stars out of cheese slices.

Star Sandwiches

Let your children help make open-faced Star Sandwiches by spreading soft cream cheese on slices of whole-wheat bread. Have the children place open star-shaped cookie cutters on top of their sandwiches and fill them with alfalfa sprouts. Then let the children remove their cookie cutters to reveal the star designs on their bread.

Fun with Many Shapes

Shape Garden

Hang a long sheet of light-colored butcher paper on a wall at your children's eye level. Cut a long rectangular window-box shape out of dark-colored paper to fit across the bottom of the butcher paper. Use a green crayon to draw stems coming out of the window box, at least one stem for each child. Finally, cut several sizes and kinds of shapes (see illustration) out of various colors of construction paper. Let each child select several shapes to glue on a small paper plate to make a flower. As each child finishes, have him or her glue the paper-plate flower to the top of a stem on the butcher paper. Have the children add leaves to the stems with crayons or more glued-on shapes.

Playdough Shapes

Set out playdough, rolling pins, plastic knives, and cookie cutters in familiar shapes. Let your children use the materials to make as many shapes as possible. Help them name the shapes as they make them.

Hint: If you do not have cookie cutters in familiar shapes, cut the desired shapes out of cardboard. Show your children how to place the shapes on flattened playdough and cut around them with a plastic knife.

Art Shapes

Give each of your children a piece of paper with a shape cut out of it. (From one paper to the next, vary the kind of shape you cut out, its size, and its location.) Ask the children to name the shapes that are cut out of their papers. Then let them draw or paint on their papers. You may wish to encourage the children to draw around the cutout shapes or to incorporate the cutout shapes into their artwork.

Shape Rubbings

Cut small familiar shapes out of thin cardboard. Put a loop of tape, rolled sticky side out, on the back of each shape. Give each of your children several shapes. Let the children arrange their cardboard shapes on a tabletop any way they wish. Have them press down on their shapes so they will stay in place. Then give each child a piece of thin paper to lay over his or her shapes. Show the children how to rub across their papers with the sides of crayons to make rubbings of the shapes. Let the children rearrange the shapes and make as many rubbings as they wish.

Mirror Shapes

Cut various sizes of familiar shapes out of plastic ribbon. Set out a mirror and the plastic-ribbon shapes. One at a time, let the children arrange and rearrange the shapes on the mirror any way they wish. Encourage them to make pictures with the shapes.

Shape Bags

Cut familiar shapes out of sponges. Make paint pads by folding paper towels in half, placing them in shallow containers, and pouring small amounts of tempera paint on them. Give your children small paper bags and the sponge shapes. Show them how to gently press their sponge shapes on the paint pads and then on their bags. Have them cover their bags with prints. Allow the paint to dry. Let the children use their bags to carry home precut paper shapes.

Shape Stickers

Make your own Shape Stickers by combining 1 package unflavored gelatin, 2 tablespoons fruit juice, and a pinch of sugar in a small saucepan. Heat just until the gelatin is completely dissolved. Use a paintbrush to paint the mixture on sheets of paper. Allow the mixture to dry. Cut the papers into familiar shapes. Give each of your children several stickers and a plain piece of paper. Let the children lick their stickers, then stick them on their papers.

Variation: Cut familiar shapes out of different colors and patterns of self-stick paper for your children to press on their papers.

Shape Houses

Set out construction-paper squares, rectangles, and triangles in a variety of sizes and colors. Give each of your children a large sheet of construction paper and some glue. Let the children select the shapes they want and experiment with placing them on their papers to create houses. When they are satisfied with their arrangements, have them glue their shapes in place. Then let them use felt-tip markers or crayons to add details as they wish.

Making Faces

Cut various sizes of familiar shapes out of different colors of felt, including one large white circle. Put the shapes in a box in front of a flannelboard. Let your children take turns arranging the shapes on the flannelboard to make clown faces.

Magnetic Shapes

Cut the following shapes out of heavy paper: squares, circles, and hearts. Attach a small piece of magnetic strip to the back of each shape. Set out non-aluminum baking pans that are the same shapes: square, round, and heart-shaped. Pass out the shape magnets to your children. One at a time, have them name their shapes and place them on the matching pans.

Sandpaper Shapes

Cut familiar shapes out of sandpaper, one for each of your children (duplicate shapes as necessary). Glue each shape to a large index card. Show the cards to the children. Ask them to close their eyes tightly while you pass out a card to each of them. Have them feel the shapes on their cards with their fingers. Ask them to guess which shapes they are touching. Then let the children open their eyes and see if their guesses were right.

Pegboard Shape Outlines

Set out a piece of pegboard with any rough edges sanded or taped. Paint familiar shape outlines on the board by "connecting the dots." Let your children take turns placing golf tees in the holes along the shape outlines.

Rubber-Band Design Board

Find a small square of plywood. Smooth out any rough edges. Hammer nails in a gridlike pattern, 1 inch apart, all over the plywood square. Give the board to one of your children, along with a variety of different sizes and colors of rubber bands. Have the child stretch the rubber bands around the nails to form familiar shapes.

Shape Picture Cards

Select 12 index cards. On four of the cards, draw pictures of triangular objects (a clown hat, an ice-cream cone, a fir tree, a coat hanger, etc.) On four other cards, draw pictures of circular objects (a face, a clock, a balloon, a ball, etc.). On the four remaining cards, draw pictures of square objects (a box, an alphabet block, a window, a soda cracker, etc.). Sit together with your children. Lay out three cards containing matching-shaped pictures and one card containing a picture that is shaped differently. Ask the children to identify the picture that is different and to tell why it does not belong with the other three. Continue, using other combinations of cards.

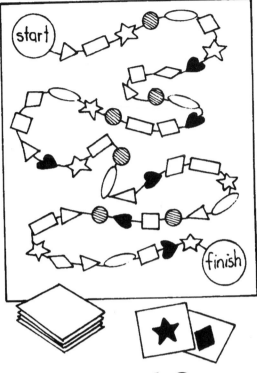

Shape Board Game

Make a game board for each group of two or three children. In the upper left-hand corner of a large piece of construction paper, draw a circle and print "Start" inside of it. Then draw a pathway of familiar shapes in random order, winding around the paper. End with a circle in the lower right-hand corner marked "Finish." Make three or four game cards for each shape by drawing the shapes on index cards. Put the cards in a pile face down and give each of your children a different kind of game marker to place on the "Start" circle. As each child turns up a card, have the child move his or her marker to the next shape designated by the card. Have the children continue playing until everyone has reached the "Finish" circle.

Guessing Game

Cut four different shapes out of construction paper. Have your children sit in a circle and place the shapes in the middle. Ask one child to close his or her eyes. Have another child take one of the construction-paper shapes and hide it behind his or her back. Ask the first child to open his or her eyes and guess which shape is missing. Continue playing the game until each child has had a chance to hide a shape and to guess which shape is missing.

Sewing Shapes

Cut heavy paper into squares. Punch holes in the outline of a familiar shape on each square. Give each of your children one of the squares and a plastic needle threaded with a piece of yarn. Show the children how to sew their shapes by pushing their needles up through one of the holes and down through the next.

Extension: Use these shapes for a feeling game. Have your children close their eyes, touch the outlines of the holes, and try to identify the different shapes.

Shape Stories

Use familiar shapes to create simple "story lines" for your children to "read." Have the children assign a word to each shape. Then let them decode the stories however they wish, using additional words between the shapes to connect the story ideas. For example, write out a symbol story like the one in the illustration below.

One child might "read" the story something like this: "A father took his child to the playground to ride on the swings and swim in the pool. Then they went home." Another child might read the story like this: "The big engine pulled the little caboose over the mountain. The moon was shining when they arrived at the next station." Start by writing short one-line stories. Then gradually create longer symbol stories, like the one below, for your children to have fun decoding.

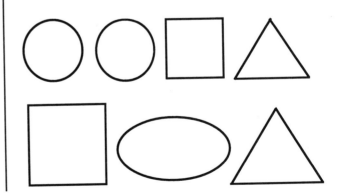

Shape Picture Books

Make a book for each of your children by stapling pieces of plain paper together with a construction-paper cover. Print "My Shape Book" and the child's name on the front. Label the pages of the book with drawings of a circle, a square, a triangle, and a rectangle. Set out precut magazine pictures of objects that are round, square, triangular, and rectangular. Help the children identify the shapes on the pages of their books. Then let them choose the matching-shaped pictures they want and glue them on the appropriate pages.

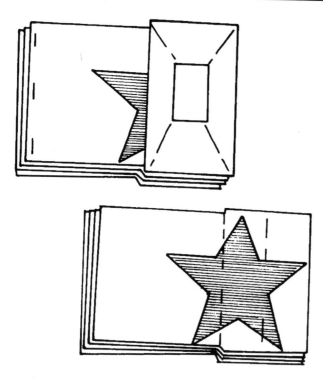

Mystery Shape Book

Cut 2 inches off the tops of several paper lunch bags that you have left folded flat. Stack the bags on top of one another with all the flaps folded on the right. Then staple the bags together on the left-hand side to make a book. Use felt-tip markers to draw a shape under each flap so that only part of the shape is visible when the flap is closed. As your children look through the book, have them look at the part of each shape that is showing and try to guess what shape is hidden beneath the flap before lifting it up.

Humpty Dumpty Shapes

Cut the following shapes out of felt: one large oval (Humpty Dumpty), one large rectangle (wall), two small circles (eyes), one small triangle (nose), one medium triangle (hat), one small oval (mouth). Arrange the shapes on a flannelboard to make Humpty Dumpty. Recite "Humpty Dumpty" with your children, taking the felt pieces off the flannelboard after the word *fall*. At the end of the rhyme, have the children "try to put Humpty together again" by arranging the felt pieces on the flannelboard. Encourage the children to name the shapes as they use them.

I Found a Shape

Out of felt, cut a large circe, a small circle, a large square, a small square, and a small triangle. Then say the rhyme below, arranging the shapes on a flannelboard as indicated.

I found a little circle,
(Place small circle on flannelboard.)

And what do you know?

My little circle started to grow.
(Place large circle on top of small circle.)

I found a great big square,
(Place large square on flannelboard.)

And what do you think?

My great big square started to shrink.
(Remove large square and put on small square.)

I found a little triangle
(Place triangle on flannelboard.)

And what do you say?

My little triangle ran away.
(Remove triangle.)

Jean Warren

Variation: Substitute three other familiar shapes for the ones in the rhyme. Or cut a set of construction-paper shapes for each of your children. Have the children hold up the appropriate shapes as you recite the rhyme.

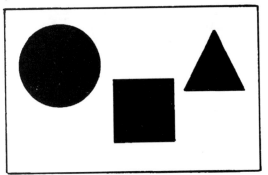

Shape Surprise Book

Punch three holes down the left-hand side of six sheets of plain paper and put them together with brass paper fasteners. Use a craft knife to cut a small square shape through all six pages. Fold back the first page and cut a triangular shape through the remaining five pages. Repeat, cutting out a round shape through pages three to six, a rectangular shape through pages four to six, a heart shape through pages five and six, and an oval shape through page six. Attach a clear-plastic page protector behind the sixth page. Cut several full-page pictures out of magazines. Insert one of the pictures in the plastic page protector. Let your children look through the cutout shapes as they turn each page. Have them try to guess what picture will be revealed when all the cutout pages have been turned. Then insert a new picture in the plastic page protector and let them try again.

Shape Bubbles

Give each of your children a pipe cleaner. Show the children how to bend the top halves into various shapes to make bubble wands. Ask the children to predict what shapes the bubbles made with their wands will be. Then let them use their bubble wands to blow bubbles. Have them notice the shapes of the bubbles. Did the shapes of the wands change the shapes of the bubbles? Let them experiment with as many shapes as they wish.

Testing Shapes for Wheels

Have your children test different shapes to see which one makes the best wheel. Cut familiar shapes, including a circle, out of cardboard. Push an unsharpened pencil or small dowel through each shape for an axle. Let the children roll the pencils across a tabletop. Which pencil rolls the easiest? Why? Which shape makes the best wheel?

Shape Hike

Make a survey form for your children to use when they go on a Shape Hike. To make the form, print "Shapes We Saw" at the top of a piece of paper. Down the left-hand side of the paper, draw four or five familiar shapes that the children will most likely see on a walk outside (square, circle, rectangle, triangle, diamond). Attach the form to a clipboard. Take the clipboard with you on the Shape Hike. Whenever the children see a shape, have them tell you. Then put a check mark next to that shape on the survey form. After you return from the hike, have the children look at the results of their survey form. Ask them questions such as these: "How many triangles did you see? How many squares? Did you see any ovals? Which shape did you see most often?"

Sun Shapes

Cut familiar shapes out of heavy paper and attach a loop of tape, rolled sticky side out, to the back of each one. Set pieces of dark construction paper in direct sunlight. Let your children attach the shapes to their papers to make designs. Ask the children to predict what will happen as the sun shines on their papers all day long. At the end of the day, have the children remove the shapes and observe what has happened to their papers. Which parts are lighter than others? Why?

Note: This experiment works best where direct sunlight is available for at least several hours.

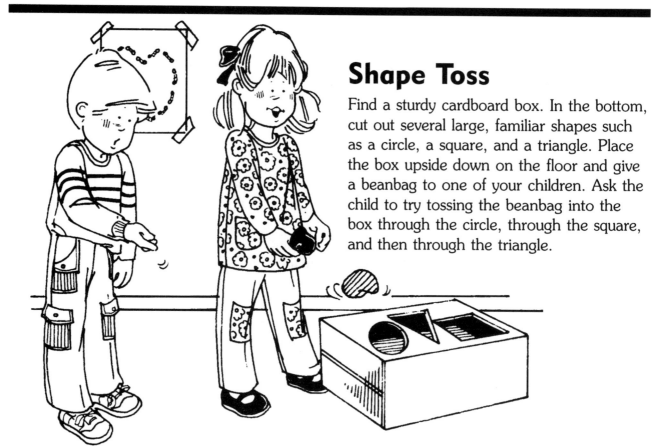

Shape Toss

Find a sturdy cardboard box. In the bottom, cut out several large, familiar shapes such as a circle, a square, and a triangle. Place the box upside down on the floor and give a beanbag to one of your children. Ask the child to try tossing the beanbag into the box through the circle, through the square, and then through the triangle.

Marching on Shapes

Help your children arrange carpet mats in the outline of a familiar shape. Put on some music and let the children march around the carpet mats, tracing the shape with their feet. Stop the music and have the children outline another shape with their carpet mats.

Shape Commands

Cut a large square and a large circle out of construction paper. Explain to your children that when you hold up the circle, they should do jumping jacks and that when you hold up the square, they should run in place. Then hold up one of the shapes and have the children do that exercise until you hold up the other shape. Continue changing from one shape to the other, giving no verbal directions. Add new shapes for different exercises as the children are ready.

Musical Shapes

Set out chairs, one for each of your children, in two rows facing back to back. Tape construction-paper shapes to the chairs. Play some music and let the children walk around the chairs. When the music stops, have them find chairs to sit on. Then let each of them name the shape on his or her chair. Continue as long as interest lasts.

Variation: Cut large shapes out of self-stick paper and place them on the floor in a circle. Have your children walk around the circle while the music plays, then stand on the shapes nearest them when the music stops.

Sing a Song of Shapes

Sung to: "Sing a Song of Sixpence"

Sing a song of shapes,
Find them everywhere.
Sing a song of shapes,
Draw them in the air.
When you look for shapes
Hiding all around,
You will see a lot of shapes
Are waiting to be found!

Gayle Bittinger

Shape Song

Sung to: "Frere Jacques"

One equal square, one equal square,
Shaped like a window, shaped like a box.
Four equal sides,
Four equal corners,
One equal square, one equal square.

One long rectangle, one long rectangle,
Shaped like a book, shaped like a door.
Two long sides,
Two short sides,
One long rectangle, one long rectangle.

One slanted triangle, one slanted triangle,
Shaped like a sail, shaped like a tree.
It has three sides,
It has three corners,
One slanted triangle, one slanted triangle.

One round circle, one round circle,
Shaped like a wheel, shaped like a plate.
One curved line
That goes round and round,
One round circle, one round circle.

Rita Choiniere

I Have a Shape

Sung to: "Skip to My Lou"

I have a square shape,
How about you?
I have a square shape,
How about you?
I have a square shape,
How about you?
Hold up your square—like I do!

Pass out paper square shapes to your children. Have everyone hold up their squares while singing the song. Repeat for as many different shapes as desired.

Jean Warren

What Shape Is This?

Sung to: "The Muffin Man"

Do you know what shape this is,
What shape this is, what shape this is?
Do you know what shape this is
I'm holding in my hand?

Sing the song several times, holding up a different shape each time. Have your children name the shape at the end of the song.

Judy Hall

Our Shapes

Sung to: "Did You Ever See a Lassie?"

Did you ever see a circle,
A circle, a circle?
Did you ever see a circle?
It looks like a ball.

Did you ever see a rectangle,
Rectangle, rectangle?
Did you ever see a rectangle?
It looks like a door.

Did you ever see a triangle,
Triangle, triangle?
Did you ever see a triangle?
It looks like a sail.

Did you ever see a square,
A square, a square?
Did you ever see a square?
It looks like a box.

Did you ever see an oval,
An oval, an oval?
Did you ever see an oval?
It looks like an egg.

Did you ever see a diamond,
A diamond, a diamond?
Did you ever see a diamond?
It looks like a kite.

Did you ever see a heart,
A heart, a heart?
Did you ever see a heart?
It looks like a valentine.

Did you ever see a star,
A star, a star?
Did you ever see a star?
It looks like a sea star.

As your children become familiar with this song, let them add their own ending to each verse.

Priscilla M. Starrett

Draw It in the Air

Sung to: "The Mulberry Bush"

This is a diamond as you can see,
   (Draw a diamond in the air with your finger.)
You can see, you can see.
This is a diamond as you can see.
Now draw it in the air with me.

Repeat for other shapes.

Neoma Kreuter

Shape Song

Sung to: "The Muffin Man"

Adult:

Oh, do you know a circle and a square,

A circle and a square, a circle and a square?

Oh, do you know a circle and a square,

A triangle and rectangle, too?

Children:

Oh, yes, we know a circle and a square,

A circle and a square, a circle and a square.

Oh, yes, we know a circle and a square,

A triangle and rectangle, too.

Adult:

Oh, do you know a diamond and a heart,

A diamond and a heart, a diamond and a
   heart?

Oh, do you know a diamond and a heart,

A star and an oval, too?

Children:

Oh, yes, we know a diamond and a heart,

A diamond and a heart, a diamond and a
   heart.

Oh, yes, we know a diamond and a heart,

A star and an oval, too.

Evelyn Smith

The Shapes Are on the Floor

Sung to: "The Farmer in the Dell"

The shapes are on the floor,

The shapes are on the floor.

Pick one up and say its name,

And then we'll pick up more.

Place a variety of paper shapes on the floor.
As you sing the song, have each of your children
pick up a shape. At the end of the song, have
each child name his or her shape, then put it
back on the floor.

Lindsay Hall

Puzzling Shapes

Clean a large, thick carrot and a zucchini. Cut the carrot and zucchini crosswise into thin circles. Use a canape cutter (available at kitchen stores) to cut a small familiar shape out of each carrot and zucchini circle. Put the shapes back into the circles. Give each of your children several of the circles with cutout shapes. Let the children take the shapes in and out. Ask them to name the shapes cut out of their circles.

Variation: Instead of a carrot and a zucchini, select light- and dark-colored bread slices. Toast the bread and use cookie cutters to cut familiar shapes out of the centers.

Finger-Gelatin Shapes

Place 1 cup grape juice in a large bowl. Sprinkle 4 envelopes unflavored gelatin over the juice. Let stand for 1 minute. Heat 3 more cups of grape juice to boiling and pour the boiling juice into the gelatin mixture. Stir until gelatin is dissolved. Pour mixture into a greased 9-by-13-inch baking pan. Chill at least 3 hours, until gelatin is firm. Use a sharp knife or cookie cutters to cut the finger gelatin into familiar shapes. Makes 4 to 5 dozen 2-inch shapes.

Variation: Instead of grape juice, use unsweetened apple juice or other clear juice. (Citrus juices do not work.)

Shape Sandwiches

Give each of your children a buttered slice
of bread. Set out cookie cutters in familiar
shapes. Let each child choose one of the
cookie cutters to cut a shape out of his
or her bread slice. Then give each child a
second slice of buttered bread and a slice
of cheese. Have the children put their sandwiches together with the cutout slices of
bread on top to make Shape Sandwiches.

Shape Pizzas

Set out pizza sauce, round English muffins
(toasted), rectangular cheese slices, round
pepperoni slices, round olive slices, triangular pineapple tidbits, green-pepper squares,
and any other toppings your children like
(cut into familiar shapes). Let the children
make Shape Pizzas by brushing pizza sauce
on the muffins, placing cheese slices on top
of the sauce, and adding toppings as desired. Bake the pizzas on a baking sheet at
350°F until the cheese is melted.

Totline® PUBLICATIONS

THEME CALENDARS
Activities for every day.
Toddler Theme Calendar
Preschool Theme Calendar
Kindergarten Theme Calendar

TIME TO LEARN
Ideas for hands-on learning.
Colors • Letters • Measuring •
Numbers • Science • Shapes •
Matching and Sorting • New Words
• Cutting and Pasting •
Drawing and Writing • Listening •
Taking Care of Myself

Teacher Resources

ART SERIES
Ideas for successful art experiences.
Cooperative Art
Special Day Art
Outdoor Art

BEST OF TOTLINE® SERIES
Totline's best ideas.
Best of Totline Newsletter
Best of Totline Bear Hugs
Best of Totline Parent Flyers

BUSY BEES SERIES
Seasonal ideas for twos and threes.
Fall • Winter • Spring • Summer

CELEBRATIONS SERIES
Early learning through celebrations.
Small World Celebrations
Special Day Celebrations
Great Big Holiday Celebrations
Celebrating Likes and Differences

CIRCLE TIME SERIES
Put the spotlight on circle time!
Introducing Concepts at Circle Time
Music and Dramatics at Circle Time
Storytime Ideas for Circle Time

EMPOWERING KIDS SERIES
Positive solutions to behavior issues.
Can-Do Kids
Problem-Solving Kids

EXPLORING SERIES
Versatile, hands-on learning.
Exploring Sand • Exploring Water

FOUR SEASONS
Active learning through the year.
Art • Math • Movement • Science

JUST RIGHT PATTERNS
8-page, reproducible pattern folders.
Valentine's Day • St. Patrick's Day •
Easter • Halloween • Thanksgiving •
Hanukkah • Christmas • Kwanzaa •
Spring • Summer • Autumn •
Winter • Air Transportation • Land
Transportation • Service Vehicles
• Water Transportation • Train
• Desert Life • Farm Life • Forest
Life • Ocean Life • Wetland Life
• Zoo Life • Prehistoric Life

KINDERSTATION SERIES
Learning centers for kindergarten.
Calculation Station
Communication Station
Creation Station
Investigation Station

1•2•3 SERIES
Open-ended learning.
Art • Blocks • Games • Colors •
Puppets • Reading & Writing •
Math • Science • Shapes

1001 SERIES
Super reference books.
1001 Teaching Props
1001 Teaching Tips
1001 Rhymes & Fingerplays

PIGGYBACK® SONG BOOKS
New lyrics sung to favorite tunes!
Piggyback Songs
More Piggyback Songs
Piggyback Songs for Infants
and Toddlers
Holiday Piggyback Songs
Animal Piggyback Songs
Piggyback Songs for School
Piggyback Songs to Sign
Spanish Piggyback Songs
More Piggyback Songs for School

PROJECT BOOK SERIES
*Reproducible, cross-curricular project
books and project ideas.*
Start With Art
Start With Science

REPRODUCIBLE RHYMES
*Make-and-take-home books for
emergent readers.*
Alphabet Rhymes • Object Rhymes

SNACKS SERIES
Nutrition combines with learning.
Super Snacks • Healthy Snacks •
Teaching Snacks • Multicultural Snacks

TERRIFIC TIPS
Handy resources with valuable ideas.
Terrific Tips for Directors
Terrific Tips for Toddler Teachers
Terrific Tips for Preschool Teachers

THEME-A-SAURUS® SERIES
Classroom-tested, instant themes.
Theme-A-Saurus
Theme-A-Saurus II
Toddler Theme-A-Saurus
Alphabet Theme-A-Saurus
Nursery Rhyme Theme-A-Saurus
Storytime Theme-A-Saurus
Multisensory Theme-A-Saurus
Transportation Theme-A-Saurus
Field Trip Theme-A-Saurus

TODDLER RESOURCES
Great for working with 18 mos–3 yrs.
Playtime Props for Toddlers
Toddler Art

Parent Resources

A YEAR OF FUN SERIES
Age-specific books for parenting.
Just for Babies • Just for Ones •
Just for Twos • Just for Threes •
Just for Fours • Just for Fives

LEARN WITH PIGGYBACK® SONGS
*Captivating music with
age-appropriate themes.*
Songs & Games for…
Babies • Toddlers • Threes • Fours
Sing a Song of…
Letters • Animals • Colors • Holidays
• Me • Nature • Numbers

LEARN WITH STICKERS
*Beginning workbook and first reader
with 100-plus stickers.*
Balloons • Birds • Bows • Bugs •
Butterflies • Buttons • Eggs • Flags •
Flowers • Hearts • Leaves • Mittens

MY FIRST COLORING BOOK
*White illustrations on black back-
grounds—perfect for toddlers!*
All About Colors
All About Numbers
Under the Sea
Over and Under
Party Animals
Tops and Bottoms

PLAY AND LEARN
Activities for learning through play.
Blocks • Instruments • Kitchen
Gadgets • Paper • Puppets • Puzzles

RAINY DAY FUN
*This activity book for parent-child fun
keeps minds active on rainy days!*

RHYME & REASON STICKER WORKBOOKS
*Sticker fun to boost
language development and
thinking skills.*
Up in Space
All About Weather
At the Zoo
On the Farm
Things That Go
Under the Sea

SEEDS FOR SUCCESS
*Ideas to help children develop
essential life skills for future success.*
Growing Creative Kids
Growing Happy Kids
Growing Responsible Kids
Growing Thinking Kids

Posters
Celebrating Childhood Posters
Reminder Posters

Puppet Pals
Instant puppets!
Children's Favorites • The Three Bears
• Nursery Rhymes • Old MacDonald
• More Nursery Rhymes • Three
Little Pigs • Three Billy Goats Gruff •
Little Red Riding Hood

Manipulatives
CIRCLE PUZZLES
African Adventure Puzzle

LITTLE BUILDER STACKING CARDS
Castle • The Three Little Pigs

Tot-Mobiles
*Each set includes four punch-out,
easy-to-assemble mobiles.*
Animals & Toys
Beginning Concepts
Four Seasons

Start right, start bright!

Totline® Publications

NEW! Early Learning Resources

For Teachers

Art Series

Great ideas for exploring art with children ages 3 to 6! Easy, inexpensive activities encourage enjoyable art experiences in a variety of ways.

Cooperative Art • Outdoor Art • Special Day Art

The Best of Totline—Bear Hugs

This new resource is a collection of some of Totline's best ideas for fostering positive behavior.

Celebrating Childhood Posters

Inspire parents, staff, and yourself with these endearing posters with poems by Jean Warren.

The Children's Song
Patterns
Pretending
Snowflake Splendor
The Heart of a Child
Live Like the Child
The Light of Childhood
A Balloon
The Gift of Rhyme

Circle Time Series

Teachers will discover quick, easy ideas to incorporate into their lessons when they gather children together for this important time of the day.

Introducing Concepts at Circle Time
Music and Dramatics at Circle Time
Storytime Ideas for Circle Time

Empowering Kids

This unique series tackles behavioral issues in typical Totline fashion—practical ideas for empowering young children with self-esteem and basic social skills.

Problem-Solving Kids
Can-Do Kids

Theme-A-Saurus

Two new theme books join this popular Totline series!

Transportation Theme-A-Saurus
Field Trip Theme-A-Saurus

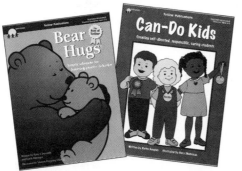

For Parents

My First Coloring Book Series

These coloring books are truly appropriate for toddlers—black backgrounds with white illustrations. That means no lines to cross and no-lose coloring fun! Bonus stickers included!

All About Colors
All About Numbers
Under the Sea
Over and Under
Party Animals
Tops and Bottoms

Happy Days

Seasonal fun with rhymes and songs, snack recipes, games, and arts and crafts.

Pumpkin Days • Turkey Days • Holly Days • Snowy Days

Little Builder Stacking Cards

Each game box includes 48 unique cards with different scenes printed on each side. Children can combine the cards that bend in the middle with the flat cards to form simple buildings or tall towers!

Castle
The Three Little Pigs

Rainy Day Fun

Turn rainy-day blahs into creative, learning fun! These creative Totline ideas turn a home into a jungle, post office, grocery store, and more!

Rhyme & Reason Sticker Workbooks

These age-appropriate workbooks combine language and thinking skills for a guaranteed fun learning experience. More than 100 stickers!

Up in Space • All About Weather • At the Zoo • On the Farm • Things That Go • Under the Sea

Theme Calendars

Weekly activity ideas in a nondated calendar for exploring the seasons with young children.

Toddler Theme Calendar
Preschool Theme Calendar
Kindergarten Theme Calendar